From Lunch Counter Protests to Corporate America

A Networking Giant Celebrating Business Stars and Saluting Black Business Hall of Fame Inductees

by

Harold D. Young

DORRANCE
PUBLISHING CO
EST. 1920
PITTSBURGH, PENNSYLVANIA 15238

Dorrance Publishing Co
585 Alpha Drive
Pittsburgh, PA 15238
Visit our website at *www.dorrancebookstore.com*

ISBN: 978-1-6491-3214-7
eISBN: 978-1-6491-3741-8

To the Founders of
The Baltimore Marketing Association, Inc.

Ackneil M. Muldrow, II
Eugene M. Smith
Gary Reynolds
John Rich
Roland Henson

TABLE OF CONTENTS

INTRODUCTION

The Civil Rights Act of 1964 became the law of the land, ending segregation in public places and banning employment discrimination on the basis of race, color, religion, sex, or national origin. That Act is considered one of the crowning legislative achievements of the Civil Rights movement.

In 1965, President Lyndon Baines Johnson's (LBJ's) Executive Order 11246 gave the law enforcement teeth.

Sit-in at the Woolworth store's lunch counter in Greensboro, N.C. in February 1960
AP Images / Atlanta Journal-Constitution

In his commencement speech at Howard University during that same year, LBJ declared, "We seek not just freedom but opportunity. We seek not just legal equity but human ability not just as a right and a theory but equality as a fact and equality as a result" (*U.S. Department of Labor, Office of Contract Compliance Programs - History of Executive Order 11246*).

Many years prior to the Civil Rights Act, intense pressure for racial equality had been growing among college and university students in the South. In 1960, it was Ackneil M. Muldrow II and some fellow students of North Carolina A & T University who staged sit-ins at a Greensboro's F.W. Woolworth Company's (a five-and-dime store) lunch counter to protest the policy that forbade African Americans from eating there. Muldrow was among the first African Americans in the nation to protest segregation of public accommodations through lunch counter sit-ins. Those protesters endured the taunts and stares of locals.

As Muldrow reflected on the stance that he and other students took, he stated, "In the end, it was worth it—not for the food but for the access."

ASCENT TO CORPORATE AMERICA

In February 1961, Muldrow left the tobacco town of Winston Salem, North Carolina to embark on a career in education, focusing his efforts primarily in the sciences. Muldrow took a temporary teaching position at Baltimore City's Booker T. Washington Middle School in March 1961, and in the fall of that year, became a full-time educator. In November 1964, after over three and a half years teaching, Muldrow learned of a management training opportunity at Montgomery Ward Department Store. Muldrow recalls that he was the first African American in the country accepted into the management training program. After joining Ward's, senior management observed Muldrow's business acumen, and soon thereafter, Muldrow was named Manager of Domestic Linens and Yard Goods.

A young professional on the move with an engaging and winning personality, Muldrow, through his social channels, pursued a position with Commercial Credit Corporation in July 1966. Muldrow consulted with his good friend and associate at Ward's, Eugene Smith ('Smitty"), knowing that Smitty had a relationship with a well-respected elected official, F. Troy Brailey, Maryland State Senator and civil rights champion. Smitty contacted Senator Brailey on behalf of Muldrow and the two men met. Senator Brailey called his contact at Commercial Credit Corporation and expressed his support for Muldrow, who was then able to compete among African American elites in Baltimore for the position of Equal Employment Opportunity Manager and ultimately was selected for the position.

The Twin-City Sentinel, Winston-Salem, N.C., reported:
"Loan Firm Promotes Winston Native"
Winston-Salem native and graduate of Atkins High School, Ackneil Muldrow, II, has been appointed coordinator of equal employment opportunity for Commercial Credit Corporation.

Muldrow, a student of the civil rights era and motivated by his personal experience of inequality, plotted for himself a self-directed career path that would equip him to succeed and gain a foothold among corporate leaders in the greater Baltimore Metropolitan Area. Muldrow used skills honed in the corporate culture to promote opportunities for other African American men and women. He initiated Commercial Credit Corporation's first Affirmative Action Program.

It was his employment at Commercial Credit Corporation that Muldrow's career and that of many other corporate executives, similarly positioned, would become an army of relationship managers that would begin fulfilling the promises of affirmative action programs born out of Title VII of the 1964 Civil Rights Act. Private corporations that received or were seeking government contracts wanted to be on the side of the law when it affected their bottom line. Leading corporations, such as Commercial Credit Corporations, Continental Can, Maryland National, and Equitable Banks, C &P Telephone Co., and Hauswald Bakery, recruited African Americans at major African American colleges and universities. Most of the African American recruits had no background in corporate America or corporate politics with which they would be confronted. Some recruits would seek refuge in fraternities and sororities, churches, and lodges. Others would find support through mentors of business enterprises and still others would develop relationships with business organizations having similar corporate experiences. Muldrow's compelling disposition and superior leadership qualities allowed him to broaden his management profile and within two years was promoted to positions of Equal Employment Opportunity Manager of Commercial Credit Company, parent company of Commercial Credit Corporation and other subsidiaries (See Appendix i, Article by Ackneil M. Muldrow, II, June 1969: A Course of Action for the Corporate Minority Relations Program).

Still not satisfied with his pace and pay at the company, Muldrow nominated himself for the position as Bank Relations and Commercial Paper Manager, where he served for three years before taking a position with Commercial Credit Industrial Company (CCIC).

National Association of Market Developers

Muldrow quickly learned that major business enterprises demanded discipline and strict adherence to a rigid corporate culture that was foreign, for the most part, to the new recruits. Through an invitation of a business associate, Muldrow would attend a meeting of an organization, which he had just recently became aware – the National Association of Market Developers (NAMD). Known neither to Muldrow, nor any of his business associates at this time, that his association with NAMD, nearly four decades later, would hold promise for a premier business organization that would be an essential link between major corporate interests, minority employment, and the minority business community in general.

NAMD was founded in 1953 and provided a safe harbor for newly- recruited corporate types. It was NAMD and the Baltimore Chapter that forged a symbiotic relationship that would bolster careers. That chapter later evolved as the Baltimore Chapter and then later known as the Baltimore Marketing Association (BMA). During that same year, the National Association of Market Developers (MAMD) was launched at Tennessee State University by Moss Kendrix as a support group for minorities in the Public Relations field.

Baltimore City had its own native son who appeared on the national stage as an aspiring professional who had carved out a role for himself among top African Americans in Sales and Marketing.

David ("Dave") J. Johnson Jr. exhibited exceptional talents in art where he competed and won two art contests by age twelve at the Walters Art Gallery and the Kiwanis Club. At his high

school alma mater, Douglass High, Dave was a member of three sports championship teams – football, boxing, and track. His confidence and exuberant personality complemented his academic excellence at Morgan State College (now University), the Academy of Fine Arts in Philadelphia, and other institutions of higher education. *Afro American Newspapers (Afro Magazine Section) February 1ˢᵗ, 1964.*

While attending Morgan, Dave was drafted into the United States Army where he served in Korea from 1950 to 1953. After receiving his degree from Morgan, he was employed by the Baltimore City Health Department as a "Food Filth" Inspector. The following year, he joined the Swift Meat Company branch office in St. Louis, Missouri as a salesman with territories throughout the continental United States, Puerto Rico, and Canada. Four years later, Dave secured a position with the National Brewing Company. According to Dave, the National Brewing, a Baltimore-based brewing company, was the home of Colt 45.

He remembers that he was in a staff meeting when discussions were held about what to name the new brewed malt liquor and he shouted, "Name it Colt after the Baltimore Colts football team!" In 1963, Jerry Hill, a popular Colts running back, was number forty-five and thus the name of the beer became, Colt 45 (*Personal Interview of David J. Johnson, Jr., November 2, 2017*). That National Brewing company became familiar to other national African American sales representatives, but it was at the Pittsburgh Courier's Home Shows where those salespersons met frequently and formulated ideas about how to advance themselves in the industry.

In an interview, Dave spoke highly of his colleague, D. Parke Gibson, President of D. Parke Gibson, International, Inc. Dave recalled how Gibson changed the paradigm about how major corporations should market products to blacks and other minorities. Gibson wrote in his book, *$70 Billion in the Black*, "Because of the growing affluence and power of non-white consumers, it will be important to the future of American and multinational firms selling to the American marketplace to learn how to sell effectively to this relatively new consumer group with its own unique set of needs and desires" (*Photograph of D. Parke Gibson reprinted from the Archives of The Baltimore Marketing Eleventh Annual Business Awards Dinner Program Booklet, December 8th, 1978*).

Dave also recalled that Leroy Jeffries and William Porter, both of whom worked at the Budweiser Company, took the lead in the early discussions of forming a national organization of sales and marketing professionals. This organization later was named the National Association of Market Developers. Dave was among the first of the Baltimore-based sales and marketing representatives to join NAMD.

In 1968, Dave landed a job in the Public Affairs Office of the Governor's Commission Law Enforcement and the Administration of Justice. A year later, he became the Director of Manpower Development and The Greater Baltimore Chamber of Commerce (later known as the Greater Baltimore Committee). As Director of New Careers, Dave worked under the Concentrated Employment Program, which was created in 1967 by Lyndon Baines Johnson's Great Society programs. Further exhibiting his concerns for social issues that affected his community, Dave was named Executive Director of the Baltimore County Community Action Agency.

In 1974, Dave became the Director of Placement and moved on to be the Director of Continuing Education at the Baltimore City Community College before retiring in 1994 (*Personal interview with David J. Johnson, Jr. Ibid.*).

NAMD was incorporated in 1954 in Washington, D.C. by Wendell P. Alston of the Esso Company, Alvin J. Talley, Raymond S. Scruggs, American Telephone and Telegraph Company (AT&T), H. Naylor Fitzhugh, an associate of the Moss Kendrix Organization, Marketing Professor of Howard University, and Vice President of Pepsi Cola Company.

However, the Baltimore Chapter of NAMD was led by a talented and diverse group of marketing and sales representatives and personnel managers who became restless because of growing tensions between the national headquarters and the local chapter. This sentiment is embodied in the modern-day theme of BMA:

"We Are More Than Just a Marketing Association," the modern-day theme of BMA has its roots deeply imbedded in the past. African American men and women who had joined major corporations in the metropolitan Baltimore area in the mid-1960s sought comradeship and

support from each other; most of these men and women found themselves, for the first time, thrust into the corporate culture, which was at once foreign and unfriendly. Corporate managers, on the other hand, dealt with the newcomers with apprehension, insensitivity and unmitigated racial prejudice. In the local Baltimore Metropolitan area, BMA provided a place of refuge for persons who had embarked on careers in sales, marketing, and personnel. However, members of BMA soon learned that they were unwittingly immersed in a broader agenda, which directed their attention beyond their corporate responsibilities.

This broader agenda and strong agenda of BMA's members allowed them to focus their attention on problems affecting African Americans in the Baltimore community. That was the proximate cause of the Baltimore Chapter of (NAMD) breaking from the national organization on September 19th, 1967. As Executive Secretary of the Baltimore Chapter, Muldrow sent a letter to Joe Black (*retired, renown Major League Baseball pitcher*), President of the National Headquarters of NAMD, which expressed the local chapter's grievances with the national organization which resulted in the birth of the Baltimore Marketing Association (BMA).

There was no specific incident that caused BMA to sever its ties with NAMD. If the separation of the two organizations could be summarized in one word, it would be accountability. Leaders in the Baltimore Chapter of NAMD complained bitterly and repeatedly to the national office that a disproportionate share of its dues was required by the National Charter to go to the national office. Members in the Baltimore Chapter argued that such disproportionality was in contravention to the trend among other national organizations. However, NAMD held fast to its Charter provision, which required local chapters to send seventy-five percent of its dues to the national office to manage the national office and operate national programs. A secondary dispute between the Baltimore Chapter and national office that fueled the tension between those two organizations was the lack of focus and support for local programming. By design the national office developed programs that it supported and looked upon local chapters to develop their programs and share with the national office the successes of their programs. However, the Baltimore Chapter remained firm about the lack of accountability and support for local programs.

Through a series of bold tactical moves, leaders in the Baltimore Chapter wrote the national office and tried to garner support for its concerns from other local chapters. Perhaps because of their allegiance, some local chapters had with the national office, and because of the lack of forceful leaders among other local chapter presidents, the Baltimore chapter stood alone and severed its relationship with NAMD.

It was the desire for change from traditional approaches that set the agenda for the five founders of BMA led by its president, John Rich, who at the time of his ascendancy to the presidency was employed as Sales Manager of the Maryland Cup Corporation. The other founders were Eugene Smith, Sales Representative for Coca-Cola Bottling Company, Gary Reynolds, assistant to Mayor, Theodore McKeldon, Roland Henson, Personnel Employment Assistant with the C & P Telephone Company, and Ackneil M. Muldrow, II, Personnel Assistant, Commercial Credit Corporation.

The founders - September 19th, 1967

Ackneil M. Muldrow, II

Gary Reynolds

John Rich, President

Eugene M. Smith

Roland Henson

Guiding these five beacons of light was the theme which read: "Our thirst for knowledge is unquestionably great…we are learning through experience and theory how businesses actually function on a day-to-day basis, with its many integral parts that mesh together to form one huge combine, known as free enterprise…we are learning our lesson well."

Mr. Joe Black
President
National Association
 Market Developers
1516 Underwood St. NW
Washington, D.C.   Sept.19,1967

Dear Mr. Black:

    After much discussion and deliberation it is the unanimous

opinion of the Baltimore membership of the National Association

of Market Developers to sever its relations with the national

body. Even though we shall continue with a program that has been

both acceptable and gratifying to our membership and community,

the Baltimore chapter can no longer in good faith operate under

 the auspices of NAMD.

                                   Sincerely,

                                   John Rich

                                   John Rich
                                   President

BMA's Legacy – The Beginning

Little did these enterprising visionaries know that in John Rich's September 19th, 1967 letter, he would sound the death knell of one organization, the Baltimore Chapter of NAMD. It also created another organization that would be the legacy organization to: (a) promote professionalism among its members, (b) support entrepreneurial pursuits of African American businesses, and (c) foster an acute recognition of the importance of encouraging youth to press forward with their educational goals and keep a keen eye on sales, marketing, and management as alternative career choices.

These founding BMA members were not short-sighted about the aspirations they had for the organization nor did their separation from NAMD result from happenstance. They laid down for themselves six principles, which would chart the course of their newly-founded organization where:

- Each BMA member must strive to improve his or her lot through professional development.
- BMA would immediately establish principles and practices of the organization and lay the foundation for a rich and enduring tradition.
- BMA members would support one another in their professional careers.
- BMA would select and pay tribute to an outstanding business and community leader each year from area businesses.
- BMA would select students for scholarships from historically black colleges and universities who showed a strong interest in careers in sales, marketing, and demonstrated financial need.
- BMA members would dedicate themselves and serve as "living witnesses" by encouraging youth in primary and secondary public schools, to (1) stay in school and (2) consider sales, marketing, and management as their career objectives.

John Rich led this new organization with his primary mission to build the membership, solicit contributions from company sponsors, and develop an appropriate organizational structure by adopting its first constitution.

Monthly meetings were held at Wilson's Restaurant (building currently owned by the Arch Social Club) at Pennsylvania and North Avenues in Baltimore.

From the beginning, as evidenced by the discussions at membership meetings, outreach to the community was the "bedrock" of BMA's programs. At the centerpiece of these programs was BMA's involvement with Baltimore City Public Schools. Distributive Education was also one of four cooperative work experience programs that brought teachers, administrators, the pupil, and the employer together. This educational program was designed to prepare students to work in the areas of selling goods and services. These students studied such topics as Marketing Functions, Store Organization, Operation and Management, Oral Expressions, Salesmanship, Store Arithmetic, and Merchandise Information.

BMA encouraged its member companies to participate in Distributive Education by providing training stations for qualified, part-time students who worked a minimum of fifteen hours per week. This program became successful because businesses immediately saw the benefits of obtaining conscientious part-time employees, provided cost savings, and fulfilled an important civic responsibility.

Structured monthly meetings provided lively exchanges among members about the direction BMA should take and the causes in which the membership should become involved. BMA's members pledged themselves to work in the community for just causes particularly those that affected the youth. Hotly debated was the issue of whether the organization would maintain its political neutrality or whether it would yield to pressures and become politically active in causes of the day. Better judgment prevailed and BMA directed its programming toward community issues that would force its membership to represent nonpartisan political views.

Two community efforts that BMA aligned themselves with were the "Project Go" and "Living Witness" programs. These programs were spearheaded and designed by employees of Westinghouse Electric Company to give junior and senior high school students the opportunities to see face-to-face, living examples of African American men and women who had gained some measures of success in their respective fields of employment. Activities of these two programs were conducted on school premises where the professionals interacted with students in their classrooms, using situational role-playing to engage students in their mentoring activities.

BMA's First Award Recipient

In 1968, Nathalia East-Roberts, a visionary BMA member, argued for and promoted the idea that BMA should recognize and celebrate the success of living black businesspersons in Baltimore.

In keeping with that vision, following one of the founding principles of the organization, BMA held its first Business Awards Dinner in December 1968. Its first Business Award recipient was Kenneth Wilson, Advertising Manager of the popular <u>Afro-American Newspapers</u>. Wilson was a former member of NAMD who had distinguished himself as an outstanding business and community leader.

His leadership qualities and business acumen were well-known in business circles, and aspiring businesspersons often sought advice from him as he willingly shared tips about his business success. Equally significant was Wilson's contribution to organizations where he frequently lent his name and services for fundraisers and served on boards of numerous community, political, and business organizations. The Awards Dinner was used for dual purposes: to recognize from the business community individuals who succeeded in business pursuits, but of equal importance, the award recipient would have to have made significant contributions to the African American community.

George Boone came to Baltimore from Memphis, Tennessee in 1941. He was the owner of Boone's Interior Decorations and Furniture and was BMA's second Business Award recipient. Boone operated several retail furniture outlets throughout Metropolitan Baltimore and was revered as an accomplished businessman. He had a tall and imposing stature and was a recognized and dependable pillar of the community. Boone's success in business was a measure of his affable and friendly temperament as a businessman who was earnestly interested in "cutting the folks in the neighborhood a deal." Residents who frequented Boone's retail stores received bargains, incentives, and special financing arrangements that were essential for young families to get their start in homemaking.

In 1948, George Boone opened Boone Furniture & Appliance Company on the first floor of a Pulaski Street storefront while his family lived in an apartment above the store. Mr. Boone sold furniture, refrigerators, appliances, and television sets, which had gained popularity in the late 1940s and early 1950s. Mr. Boone sold top-of-the-line furniture, such as Thomasville, Lane, and America of Martinsville. He also sold Maytag washing machines, Admiral television sets, RCA, and General Electric products. Boone's Furniture was the first minority-owned furniture and appliance store in Baltimore. Boone's son, Maurice, was a skilled interior decorator who operated the Liberty Road store and served as Vice President of the corporation.

In September 1969, John Rich proudly passed the gavel of leadership to Gary Reynolds, BMA's second president. Reynolds, in his position as Assistant to Mayor Theodore R. McKeldin, who directed the membership's attention toward broader community issues that had set the stage for BMA's permanent influence in community affairs in Baltimore.

Under Reynold's leadership, BMA made its first scholarship award to Shirley Stackhouse, who had matriculated at Mt. Providence Junior College. Reynolds realized that if BMA wanted to have an impact on the education of youth that scholarship awards to deserving students would have to become a top priority. As a result, the BMA Scholarship Fund was established to provide assistance to students who were pursuing careers in marketing, personnel, management, and related fields.

ACKNEIL M. MULDROW, II'S LEADERSHIP MODEL

Reynolds successfully completed a year of service as BMA's second president, and in September 1970, Ackneil M. Muldrow II, Manager of Equal Employment Opportunity for Commercial Credit Corporation, assumed the presidency.

Muldrow brought to BMA a heightened level of professionalism, produced its first annual report, possessed unbridled enthusiasm, a penchant for organizational structure, and formal lines of communication. Before his presidency, BMA was essentially run solely by its president. As its new president, Muldrow lobbied for a broader organizational structure that would significantly increase members' roles in the organization. He created vice presidents for membership, entertainment, finance, public information, and student affairs. Members used this platform of the committee vice-presidents to develop their talents that were transferrable to their various workplaces.

Discussing the future of the new organizational structure of BMA above is from L-R: Scalar Cooper (3-M Companies), Joseph Fitts III (Bethlehem Steel Corp.), Frederick A. Bailey, Jr.

Bailey (Maryland National Bank), Ackneil M. Muldrow II (Commercial Credit Corporation), and Harold D. Young (Commercial Credit Corporation).

Members frequently met between monthly meetings to plan strategies that would ultimately catapult BMA into prominence among those organizations, which supported members who were employed at major corporations as they focused on the promotion for business development among young entrepreneurs.

Under Muldrow's leadership, BMA's first annual report touted the organization's financial soundness. His contacts with African American corporate executives brought nationally-renowned speakers to address Baltimore audiences at Annual Business Awards Banquets. During his administration, he also recruited new BMA members from diverse corporate organizations, which included lending institutions, universities, utility companies, newspapers, federal, state, and local governments.

Muldrow's insight on issues affecting African Americans placed BMA on the cutting edge of social change. In his annual report, Muldrow remarked that "at this point in time, one percent of the population controls forty percent of the wealth and the bottom one-fifth of our population gets but six percent of the income [and]…as seen by the many not-so-rich, the nation's economic system appears to be welfare for the rich and free enterprise for the poor."

Muldrow, Equal Opportunity Manager, Commercial Credit Company, above in the photograph, is conversing with Travis Vauls, President of the Baltimore Urban League about his concerns of the wealth gap in the Metropolitan Baltimore community. Muldrow also chided the banking community for its reluctance to make business loans to African American businesspersons. He stated in the American Banker newspaper that "banks failure to address the needs of minority businesspersons is primarily the results of discrimination." He also said, "There has been a history of discrimination against minority businessmen in Baltimore." He explained that "banks need to show empathy for the black loan applicant and hire and train more black officials who can use their 'mother wit' to find ways to make loans to minority businessmen rather than create ways to screen-them out."

In December 1970, Raymond V. Haysbert Sr. was BMA's third Business Award honoree. Haysbert was Director, Executive Vice President, and General Manager of H. G. Parks, Inc.

His initial employment after graduating Cum Laude from Wilberforce University in Business Administration was as an instructor at Central State University in Xenia, Ohio. He was briefly employed at Veterans' Housing in Wilberforce, Ohio. Haysbert held significant and influential Board of Director positions in Baltimore that included: Business league of Baltimore, Health and Welfare Council, Economic Development Commission, Mayor's Committee on Finance, Advance Federal Saving and Loan, Baltimore Investment Council, 611 Corporation, and the Baltimore Area Council on Alcoholism.

Outside of business, Haysbert became a political adviser and community leader. He was involved with the campaign of Harry Cole, who became the first black state senator in Maryland. He also helped Henry G. Parks, Jr to win a seat on the Baltimore City Council in 1963.

It was no small wonder that Muldrow's attention, impatience with the frailties and failures of the larger business community, was drawn to seek a high-profiled business executive who had enjoyed enormous success in promoting and marketing products of the Park Sausage Company, Raymond Haysbert. He was the Vice President of the Park Sausage Company and had become a giant in the business community. Haysbert had much to say about everything marketing, politics, promoting black businesses, fundraising, and supporting community events.

Haysbert is pictured in the forefront with Henry G. Parks Jr., President and CEO of Parks Sausage Company.

When Haysbert spoke, people listened because he was well respected for his ability to sell and promote unique business concepts and could easily shift his energies toward working in the trenches with community leaders on "nuts-and- bolts" issues affecting everyday people. The success that Haysbert enjoyed as a businessman flowed from the idea that the advice he gave actually worked.

As one businessman had said, "If Ray backed an idea or a business concept, you could go to the bank with it."

FIRST SCHOLARSHIP AWARD TO
A HISTORICALLY BLACK COLLEGE

In 1970, the first student scholarship was awarded to Maggie Lane of Morgan State College (University), a historically Black College, at the Annual Awards Dinner.

Lane said that "it meant so much to me for a well-known business organization to select me for a scholarship." She continued, "BMA not only gave me the scholarship, but the gift inspired me to excel."

In 1971, BMA broke with its tradition of "political neutrality" and honored Robert Douglass, President, Baltimore Electronics Association, Incorporated, who was also a State Senator.

Some members perceived the selection of Douglass as the honoree to be a violation of BMA's stated policy against partisan politics. Others argued that Douglass was a businessman and civic leader who happened to be a state legislator. Because Douglass had established a major business in an African American community, he had the capacity to employ local residents so the majority of the membership conceded that Douglass' award was given to him primarily because he was highly recognized for his work in the electronics industry.

BMA's Economic Development Ventures

In 1972, the National Development Council (NDC) approached BMA and asked them to participate in a new economic development initiative by the U.S. Small Business Administration (SBA) 502 Program. BMA immediately seized this opportunity because the purpose of this new governmental effort was to establish a Local Development Companies (LDC's), which had successfully operated in rural areas for many years. It was designed to create and retain jobs through financing small businesses or making funds available to small business development projects.

Through SBA's 502 Program, the LDC program provided long-term financing for the fixed assets (plant, equipment, and land) of businesses and enabled commercial banks and other private lending institutions to make loans that, by normal standards, would be overlooked because the businesses lacked sufficient equity investment in their projects.

On November 24th, 1972, BMA through Muldrow's insistence and guidance, created an economic development entity, the BMA Development Corporation, a non-stock corporation for the sole purpose of leveraging BMA's participation in this economic development vehicle in Baltimore.

This LDC was a separate legal entity with a separate mission and purpose from BMA. Muldrow insisted that the only link between BMA and BMA Development Corporation was their officers who held dual positions in both organizations. The corporate members were members and non-members of BMA. In order for this venture to be launched, each interested member was requested to invest $587 in "seed" money from the BMA members and others. (Image Ownership: Public Domain)

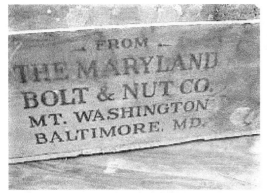

21

First Venture - Manufacturing Facility

The first venture was a $480,000 financial effort for the Leonard Jed Company to buy the plant and other assets of the old Maryland Nut and Bolt Company. On May 14th, 1973, G.J. Lang of the Small Business Administration, wrote Muldrow, Chairman of the Board, BMA Development Corporation, authorizing a direct loan to the LDC to assist Leonard Jed Company. This plant was located along the Jones Falls Expressway and was severely damaged in a hurricane in 1972.

BMA Development Corporation was responsible for ten percent of that project ($48,000) in cash or "in-kind" services. The remaining ninety percent was supposed to be financed by the SBA, a commercial bank or an insurance company. The ninety percent could have been with any combination of lenders. In this particular case, Maryland National Bank provided $200,000, the SBA financed $232,000, and BMA Development Corporation provided $48,000 in-kind contributions to the project.

The BMA Development Corporation negotiated an administrative servicing fee of one per annum. Since BMA had no administrative servicing capabilities, the fee was waived for this project. Thus, the borrower made the loan payments directly to the lender.

Second Venture - Expansion of Medical Center

In September 1973, the BMA Development Corporation participated as the LDC for the $1,150,000 Phase II expansion of Garwyn Medical Center. BMA Development's contribution was $115,000.

Our giving in-kind credits were for the architect's fees, site surveys, attorney's fees, marketing studies, etc. In actuality the doctors at Garwyn paid for these items.

On November 1st, 1973, Gregory L. Reed, Frank, Bernstein, Conaway, & Goldman, attorneys for First National Bank, wrote Lowell R. Bowen, attorney, Miles and Stockbridge, evidencing the loan of $455,000 to BMA Development Corporation for the Garwyn Medical Center. The BMA Development Corporation was the owner of the second building constructed for the medical center. That construction financing was provided by American Medical Builders Guild.

Again, since BMA had no administrative servicing capabilities, the fee was waived for this project. The borrower made the loan payments directly to the New York Life Insurance Mortgage (NYLIM) and Equitable Trust Company. The BMA development Corporation building, along with Garwyn Medical Center, were sold to Jerry Hill, a local businessman. That sale price was not disclosed. BMA transferred the ownership of the property in exchange for being released from the indebtedness.

Third Venture - Manufacturing Facility

Steel Drum Manufacturing Company (Image Ownership: Public Domain)

A Maryland Steel Drum Manufacturing Company proposal was withdrawn at the request of the owners. By 1972, President Lyndon Johnson's Great Society efforts were coming to an end. President Richard Nixon's administration was now in power and many of the programs established in the 1960s were abolished or dismantled. Unfortunately, the SBA 502 Program was also abolished.

In September 1972, BMA found Eugene Smith as its fourth president, a sales and marketing force that brought the organization to grips with one of its unspoken missions to improve specialized marketing and public relations programs that were important to United States firms, which were directly impacting the African American consumer market. Eugene Smith was a District Manager with the Coca-Cola Bottling Company in Baltimore. He was a "bottom line" manager who exacted from the BMA membership, a basic commitment to sound marketing and management principles.

Smith focused his membership drive on individuals with experience in sales and marketing. He persuaded his Vice President of Activities to fill the year's agenda with programs that promoted BMA as a marketing association. Smith warned the membership that, *"If we don't take time to learn and practice the fundamentals of marketing, the essence of what this organization is about, will slowly erode and the concepts of marketing as we know it, will be lost to rhetorical symbolism."* With the full support of his leadership team and members at large, Smith was confident with the mission of his administration and forged ahead by looking back at the principles set forth by its founders.

Thus, Pauline B. Brooks, President of Pauline Brooks Fashions, Inc. became BMA's fifth Business Award recipient.

Mrs. "B," as she was affectionately called by her models and business friends, operated a retail specialty shop and had been in some phase of business for more than two decades prior to receiving the award. Brooks developed her business from the "up-scale" African American women's market, obtaining many of her fashions from New York with international influences. Moving into the Mondawmin Mall, she became the first African American business woman to establish a modern boutique in a major shopping center.

BMA's members attend its Annual Formal Dinner Dance (circa May 1973).

In 1973, during the administration of Eugene Smith, BMA, in association with the Business League of Baltimore where Frederick Nunley was president, Smith spearheaded the formation of an alternative business development organization (BDO) for minority businesspersons. He also created this entity with the Metropolitan Business Resource Center (MERC). After some research by the outgoing president, Mr. Smith picked up that concept and worked to implement the BDO with other community resources identified by BMA.

BMA jointly approached the Greater Baltimore Committee to initiate this project with the other participants—the Business League of Baltimore, Baltimore Chamber of Commerce, Greater Baltimore Committee, and the Baltimore Urban Coalition.

After some deception by the GBC and others, the MBRC became operational, and its headquarters was located at 330 North Charles Street. The purpose of this venture was to provide business counselling, loan packaging, management, technical assistance, and other business-related services.

The initial funding of $100,000 for the BRC came from a grant by the U.S. Department of Commerce through John Jenkins, who headed the Office of Minority Business Enterprise (OMBE). The first executive director of that agency was James Workman. He was followed by Pickett Thomas, Phillip Brown, and Mary Beth Banks. The MERC operated for five years.

However, one missing ingredient of the entire operation was its inability to network and identify procurement opportunities. During the operation of the MBRC, a board member, the late Herman L. Carter, successfully lobbied the National Supplier Development Council to establish a component organization under the umbrella of the MBRC.

The Metropolitan Baltimore Minority Purchasing Council (MBMPC) was then given the charge to identify procurement opportunities for minority businesses, and they matched the partners with major corporations in the region. The MBRC was successful in managing the only purchasing counsel of its type in the entire region.

When federal funds for minority initiative programs became scarce, the GBC, the Chamber and the Urban Coalition, picked up the funding. On or about 1979, the sponsoring organizations withdrew funding because funding in their own organizations was questionable. Mr. Carter fought hard to have a separate organization established, of which BMA did not choose to be involved. Thus, the Baltimore Purchasing Council was formed as the forerunner of the Maryland/D.C. Supplier Development Council.

In September 1974, James Waller, at the age of twenty-eight, the youngest BMA member, ascended to the top leadership position and became BMA's fifth President. While the prior administration reinforced the basic marketing principles, the BMA membership wanted to integrate those foundational principles with new insight from Waller, who felt compelled to energize the youth among the local black colleges and universities.

James Waller was a young account executive with Connecticut General Life Insurance Company and was on the "fast track" to success in the insurance industry. He used his "insider" expertise in management and ushered in new ideas, programs, and infectious enthusiasm.

Waller's youthfulness was a "big hit" with college and university students. During his two-year term, his theme became "rhetoric vs. reality." He also wanted to make certain that college students clearly understood what they were up against upon graduation.

James Waller and his leadership team spent a fair amount of time lecturing at institutions of higher education and adopted as a special project, the Society for Advancement of Marketing (SAM) on Morgan State University's campus. Waller told the SAM organization during one of his lectures that the graduates and his meet some of the most difficult challenges in the business world. He said, *"Those of you who dare to become entrepreneurs, beware that mere competition causes many businesses to fail before the end of the first year of operation… and those of you who will venture up the corporate ladder, remember that the jobs that you will compete for are the same jobs that are traditionally reserved for white males."*

Barbara Johnson (Earl) had extensive institutional knowledge of BMA and was elected as the First Vice President to Waller. Drawing on her background in corporate management at C&P Telephone Company, Earl had the skills to "steady the ship," which gave Waller the support and time he needed to reach out and nurture relationships with the collegiate community.

Waller's association with Morgan brought him in contact with Dr. Winfred O. Bryson, head of Morgan's Business Department.

Dr. Bryson was a well-respected educator but was best known because he was the President of Advance Federal Savings and Loan (S&L) Association. As compared to most of the larger S&L's, Advance had modest assets. Nonetheless, Advance made more mortgage loans as a percentage of its assets in the inner city than most other leading institutions. It was for that reason Waller said, *We felt that he was clearly the best candidate for the BMA Business Award - he is our unsung hero.* Dr. Bryson was the sixth BMA Awards recipient.

Dr. Bryson's commitment to making inner city mortgage loans was particularly significant because it was evident during this period that other lending institutions had "red-lined" inner city neighborhoods; they favored loans to persons living on the periphery of the city and county.

After speaking with BMA's membership with unbridled enthusiasm and fervent support for Dr. Bryson, Waller then tapped Zerita Thornton to chair the BMA Awards Dinner. Thornton was a capable C & P Telephone Company manager. She was known for her planning skills and produced an eventful evening that culminated in Dr. Bryson receiving the honor of high distinction among his peers.

Pamela Fields was a WBAL-TV personality and became BMA's seventh honoree. Fields was a pioneer in the Baltimore television market. Equally impressive was her community involvement and special charities that she regularly supported. Fields left the Baltimore area with pleasant memories of a very special person who was, at one time, Baltimore's own.

 In 1975, Helen Stafford was the first woman president of BMA and the first entrepreneur to serve at the helm. Stafford's entrepreneurial interest peaked the membership's awareness of the struggles among small minority businesses. She was President of the Career Development Corporation (CDC) and Driving School. One division of CDC was an apprenticeship program funded through the U.S Department of Labor. It was through this contract that printing contract apprentices were trained. This effort lead to the printing and publishing of The Business Compendium, BMA's first newsletter and was edited by Harold D. Young, BMA Vice President. It was a quarterly publication that presented business and economic news that focused on issues impacting the African American community.

Business Compendium...Excerpt

BALTIMORE MARKETING ASSOCIATION, INC.
4718 LIBERTY HEIGHTS AVE. BALTIMORE, MD 21215
VOLUME I NUMBER I   FALL 1975

EDITOR'S NOTE

Harold D. Young

This is the first issue of The Business Compendium, published quarterly by the Baltimore Marketing Association, Inc.

Geared primarily to the minority business community, this quarterly will endeavor to present in summary form a collection of materials representing a wide range of business activity. To this end, The Business Compendium will function as a business informational clearing house through which business and economic issues affecting minority business persons are given public exposure. In furtherance of the organization's goal of professional enrichment, this publication will serve as a news medium that responds positively to the exchange of ideas among persons having diverse interests...

State of BMA

By Helen Stafford, President

The Baltimore Marketing Association, a professional organization, continues to serve the community through its efforts to create business and scholastic awareness. Through the exchange of experience and knowledge, BMA offers its expertise to those who seeks its services.

BMA's wings of knowledge and experience also expand outside of the business community and into the field of education. Members of our organization address colleges and universities on factual aspects of the business world, in an attempt distinguish "rhetoric from reality." To fulfill the great needs of the Black entrepreneur, BMA is a sponsor of the Business the Metropolitan Business Resource Center. BRC, a federally funded program is designed to assist entrepreneurs in all phases of business operations. One of BRC's most successful projects is the Annual Trade Fair that assist small businesses to exhibit their products before major corporations...

Under Helen Stafford's administration, she promoted small business seminars and developed a following of business owners who built the support within the organization for the selection of E. Gaines Lansey, who on December 5th, 1975, became BMA's eighth Business Award honoree. Lansey was the President of Ideal Savings on Druid Hill Avenue. He was a prominent leader in Baltimore and gave generously of his time to Provident Hospital, YMCA, and other community-based organizations.

Lansey put real meaning in neighborhood banking. He personally serviced loans and knew most of his customers by their first names.

In 1975, Ideal Savings and Loan Association was the oldest black banking institution in the city of Baltimore. Although Lansey was personable with his customers, he was, nonetheless, a hard-nosed businessman.

In the summer of 1976, during an interview with Lansey, published by The Business Compendium, he reported that he only had one loan that he had not collected. He said, *"I made loans simply on a person's ability to pay and then I serviced the loans with the idea that if a borrower had the desire to repay the loan, I'd find out a way to help him… No other association in town is willing to service small yield loans."*

BMA Salutes The Bicentennial Celebration

In 1976, Baltimore and the rest of the nation celebrated the Bi-Centennial and in its Bi-Centennial publication, BMA gave its salute:

The Baltimore Marketing Association joins the Greater Baltimore Community in commemorating the 200th birthday of our nation.

Basic to the freedoms for which the American Revolution was fought, blacks' struggle for individual rights and self-determination, also has its roots deeply imbedded in the history of this country.

Founders of BMA were motivated in 1967 to organize its members to address the social, political, and economic forces which historically prohibited blacks from advancing in the ranks of major corporations and also retarded the number of blacks entering into self-employment. The crippling effects of this unequal treatment spirited the early organizers of BMA to stage a series of discussion forums. As these discussions progressed, an obvious fact emerged was that while change is inevitable, it was difficult to come by, especially as it involved corporate managers whose attitudes had crystallized over the years. So BMA approached the problem by developing strength from within the ranks of the organization.

As the revolution progresses, so continues the struggle of blacks and other minorities to share equally in the wealth of this nation. To the members of BMA, the celebration of 1976 marks an end of a significant period in history and a beginning of vision where the freedom of entrepreneurs to enter into business is restricted only by the competitive forces of the market place and where all individuals, regardless of race, sex, age or national origin, will be fairly represented in all facets of employment.

In the interest of preserving personal dignity, individual rights and the opportunity for one to exercise self-determination, the Baltimore Marketing Association pledges its support in celebrating the 1976 Bicentennial.

Following the 1976 Bi-Centennial festivities, BMA elected Harold D. Young. He was the Program Manager with the U.S. Department of Housing and Urban Development.

Young's background in government represented a major departure from the traditional work experiences of former BMA presidents.

With degrees in Economics and Urban Planning, Young's administration focused on social concerns impacting the broader community, which was contrasted with Stafford's who "tinkered" with the intricacies of how business function on a day to day basis.

In 1974 to 1975, interesting events were unfolding that BMA supported through its legislators and presence at the legislature. In July 1975, the Maryland Legislature signed into law a bill which created as a permanent agency, the Maryland State Office of Minority Business Enterprise (MSOMBE). This permanent agency status was an attempt to restructure purchasing and procurement, so that minority and small business owners would benefit from state contracting.

Another bill pursued during the same general assembly session and supported by BMA directed certain state agencies to try and achieve a goal for procurement from small and minority businesses, of ten percent of the dollar value of goods and services. The State of Maryland, during that period, was giving less than one percent of its contracts to minority businesses. An experimental program developed by the State only allowed African Americans to bid on state purchasing contracts, which involved less than $5,000. This new policy angered some white contractors who called this effort an exercise in "reverse discrimination."

Young sought to involve BMA in the minority entrepreneurial process of building the Baltimore Rapid Transit System. Organized principally by Ackneil Muldrow II, Young held a special luncheon meeting at Restaurant 3900 North Charles Street (the first time an African American group had met there). The purpose of the meeting was to stimulate BMA members to think about business opportunities for themselves and other African Americans in the construction of the Baltimore subway system, which was being planned by the state of Maryland for Baltimore City and Baltimore County.

The luncheon speaker was Mr. Charles Brown, Manager of the Affirmative Action Programs, Washington Metropolitan Transit System (Washington METRO). He shared many of the experiences of minority businesspersons in the planning and construction of the Washington D. C. system, which was being built at that time.

Messrs. Young and Muldrow met with Mr. Boucher and the late Joseph Doerr, Special Assistant of Transportation for Governor Marvin Mandel. The meeting was to discuss GBC's and the state's commitment to minority businesses in the construction of the rapid transit system. Each of them offered "hollow" commitments. As a result, BMA was asked to identify and recruit <u>local</u>, <u>experienced</u> minority businesses that could provide services to the rapid transit construction project. But BMA rejected that position since no local minority businesspersons had ever built a "damn" subway system.

Under Young's leadership, BMA honored diverse business owners. In 1976, Ann and Bernard Lacewell marked the first time that BMA featured two honorees. The Lacewells were a husband and wife team and the owners of La Cosmatique, a Fuller Products franchise, cosmetic outlet located in Mondawmin Mall.

The Lacewells were originally from New York and moved to Baltimore in 1965 to manage a branch office of Fuller. Soon thereafter they purchased the franchise and became a retail and wholesale distributor. In addition to supplying Fuller Products, the Lacewells conducted specialized cosmetology lectures and sales demonstrations.

Awards Dinner attendees, honoring the Lacwells, socialize with 1976 Awards Dinner speaker, George Brokemond, President, Highland Bank, Chicago, Illinois.

Left-George Brokemond; Center: Ruth Crowder; Right: Kenneth O. Wilson, Vice President and Advertising Manager of the Afro, Past Honoree

Pictured left, Brokemond, Ruth Crowder engage in thoughtful conversations with Kenneth O. Wilson, Advertising Executive, Afro-American Newspapers.

Otis Warren was the choice for the tenth Business Award in 1977. Warren had established himself as on outstanding businessman and realtor in Baltimore City and surrounding counties.

During this period, Warren had the largest African American sales force in a five-state area. His success was linked to the quality of training he incorporated with this professional development of each sales agent. Warren would often say to his agents, *"If you want to be a part of the Otis Warren Company, you'll have to grow with the industry, or you will perish."*

The following year in 1978, BMA named as the eleventh Business Honoree Robert Clay of Robert Clay, Inc.

Clay rose to success quickly as he competed for and won major construction contracts through the U.S. Small Business Administration (SBA) Section 8(a) Program. He provided minority and disadvantaged businesses, special dispensation to compete on federal contracts. As Chairman of the Board of the Maryland Minority Contractors Association, Clay used this organization to advance the causes of minority businesses. He was well known in Baltimore and in the Baltimore Metropolitan area for his "fire brand" style of leadership. Sanctioning his temperament, a small minority contractor remarked that "there is no federal, state, or local government agency that Bob won't call to task if they are not forthright with small and minority businesses." It was during the Business Awards Dinner honoring Robert Clay that BMA's Scholarship was memorialized in the name of John S. Sheppard, Jr.

John Sheppard was a 1973 scholarship recipient and later died in 1978. He was a Morgan State University student who graduated Magna Cum Laude in 1975. Sheppard was the first president of the Society for Advancement of Management (SAM) at Morgan. His inquisitive mind and imaginative leadership established a lasting relationship between SAM and BMA.

Melvin Bilal was the twelfth honoree. Bilal was the president of Howard Security, a firm headquartered in Howard County. It provided a broad range of security services to government agencies and private businesses. Bilal incorporated his business in 1973 and later expanded contracts for security services to Baltimore, Washington, and Southern Virginia where he landed a lucrative federal government contract. He was an astute businessman, lending his talents for social causes and fostering initiatives in the city of Baltimore that promoted business development and self-determination.

Self-determination accurately characterized BMA's eighth president, Sandra East, who was elected president in September 1980. East, for many years, served in several posts for BMA to include being Executive Secretary, where she was known for taking accurate minutes for the Board of Directors. She was also known in the greater Baltimore community for hosting lively Friday evening socials. East invited university leaders, politicians, civil rights, and government officials for important robust discussions, which affected African Americans.

After working for Westinghouse Electric Company for several years, she became the Equal Opportunity Specialist for the U.S. Customs Agency. As a government official, Sandra East respected the chain of command. During her tenure as BMA's president, she ran the organization by delegating responsibility for programs to the lowest possible level in the organization. She believed strongly that every member should be given the opportunity of leadership.

It was East's sense of fairness that caused her outrage at the promoters of the International Film Festival in 1980 because they purposefully excluded the Arena Players as one of the locations to showcase the organization's films in Baltimore. The Arena Payers was the longest continuously operating African American theater in America. East wrote several articles in the then <u>News American</u> newspapers and said: *"You have no right to come into our city and ignore the very existence of one of Baltimore's most cherished institutions…we demand an explanation and reconsideration of your decisions."* As a result of her insistence, Hope Quackenbush, one of the Festival Planners and staffers of the Morris Mechanic Theater, met with Camile Sherrod of the Arena Playhouse, and soon thereafter, joined the Board and became an active and influential member of the Board.

The dual talents of the Maddox brothers, J. Albert and Francis J., gained them prominence in the printing business (*Below, Frank and Al are busy at the print shop*).

The Maddox brothers, who became BMA's thirteenth Business Awards recipients, came from a family of who had been associated with the printing industry since their grandfather, Gabriel B. Maddox, Sr. opened the Maddox Printing in 1907. Gabriel studied under Booker T. Washington at Tuskegee Institute, Tuskegee, Alabama.

Frank and Al worked at the Afro-American Newspapers for several years until in 1954 the brothers established a new business, Time Printers Inc., so named because they wanted to assure customers that its work would be delivered on time with qualitative printing jobs, and therefore its name became synonymous with professional printing among many social and business organizations. The business began in a storefront at 2239 N. Fulton Avenue and later moved to Warwick Avenue, Baltimore, Maryland.

In 1981, there was no Business Award Banquet nor a BMA honor for any outstanding businessperson during that year. Instead East and the Board of Directors decided to use the better portion of the year to plan for the growth and future development of the organization. There had been a measurable decline in membership over the past year, which caused some of the programs and activities to suffer.

As a matter of record, it was because East recognized the need to rejuvenate the organization, that she dispatched Harold D. Young to reach out once again to Ackneil M. Muldrow II for his organizational talents. Hence in 1982, Muldrow became BMA's ninth president. Muldrow's primary mission was to produce and implement a plan that would focus the organization on its founding principles. He pulled together a cadre of leaders within and from outside of BMA and began the rebuilding process in the "old fashion way," with committed, energetic, and talented persons from diverse backgrounds. By the end of 1982, BMA had rebounded from its "temporary recession," and the new and experienced members worked earnestly together to produce impressive results.

The selection of Henry G. Parks Jr. as the fourteenth honoree reflected the new-found confidence among the members of BMA that the organization was properly positioned to forge ahead and accept the challenges that had presented themselves.

Parks was the founder and Chairman of the Board of H.G. Parks, Inc. (Parks Sausage Company). He had extensive experience in advertising, public relations, and several business enterprises prior to him founding the Parks Sausage Company. He served on national and local boards and was known for his earnest, energetic work and willingness to serve his community. Parks had a positive personality and once said that, *"You don't get anything by being negative—as a salesperson, you have to count the sales you make, not the ones you lose."* Pragmatic about the prospects for his race, Parks thoughtfully mused that *"I think we need to learn how to be managers and how to operate profitable businesses, because we will never learn how to be strong as people until we begin to have some self-sufficiency - to own, to have access to capital and the proper use of it."*

A portion of the funds raised at the Awards Dinner for Parks was distributed to the Blue Chip-In project. Through Blue Chip-In (a new venture launched by Mayor William Donald Schaefer and the business community), private companies and associations "invested" in projects that stalled due to federal budget cuts but were important to the quality of life in Baltimore. Those projects were designed to create new jobs, train unemployed persons, and to provide important services that went above and beyond the responsibilities of the government.

In 1983, BMA saluted Rudolph C. Gustus, founder and President of G & M Oil Company. At the time of the award, G & M was the nation's seventh largest minority-owned and operated business.

G & M began operating in 1963 by James Gustus and his son Rudolph with one oil truck. Gustus's climbed to success in the heating oil business. He came from hard work, marketing, and professional customer service. Gustus expanded his business with the purchase of the Texaco Oil terminal in the Fairfield section of Baltimore city. About his planned growth strategies, Gustus said, *"That we intend to become even more of a factor in Baltimore heating oil market."*

While Gustus sought to expand his market share of the Baltimore oil business, there were other forces working against the tide which undermined his efforts and those of other African American entrepreneurs. This was evidenced in the U.S. Commission on Civil Rights Hearings in Baltimore.

U.S. Commission on Civil Rights Hearings–Baltimore

In April 1983, the U.S. Commission on Civil Rights ("Commission") issued a study entitled, Greater Baltimore Commitment: A Study of Urban Economic Development. This Commission found that minority participation in the economic development in the city of Baltimore was negligible. The report stated that *"The city has many creative and innovative public and private sector leaders whose joint efforts are rapidly transforming Baltimore from a stereotype of decaying urban blight to a model metropolis frequented by tourist from around the globe…not all of Baltimore's population has been included in [Baltimore's] transformation."* At that time, minority economic development had not been a priority in Baltimore city. The report cited a range of problems in Baltimore, including the scarcity of black loan and bonding officers and the related lack of access to both commercial loans and bonds by potential black entrepreneurs.

One of the recommendations of that study was, *"The city of Baltimore and the Greater Baltimore Committee should actively encourage banks and surety houses to review their commercial lending practices and policies to ensure that minority-owned businesses have equal access to capital. In addition, these financial institutions should take affirmative steps to hire and train more minority bond and loan officers."*

On September 20th, 1982, in a telephone interview conducted by Commission examiners with  Stanley Tucker of the Maryland Small Business Development Financing Authority, Tucker announced an imitative of the Greater Baltimore Committee to *"Establish a $7.5 million loan fund to help start and expand businesses owned by social or economically deprived persons in Baltimore."*

The financial institutions that committed funds for this effort were: the Maryland National Bank, Union Trust Bank, First

National Bank of Maryland, Mercantile Bank and Trust, Equitable Trust Bank, and Suburban Trust Bank.

Fortuitously, during the hearings of the Commission that began in 1981, one of the founders of BMA, Ackneil M. Muldrow II, later tapped in 1983, to be President and CEO of the Development Fund (DCF). This organization became the principal lender for small, minority, and disadvantaged businesses in Baltimore city. DCF was established to give disadvantaged businesses access to capital throughout the Mid-Atlantic Region. Muldrow's background in bank relations as a corporate manager made him an attractive candidate for the job. His strong belief was a priority to improve the plight of the black community and its economic infrastructure-business development and living wages for its citizens.

The theme, "We are more than just a marketing association," grew its organizational legs under Muldrow's leadership with the support of minority business development and the recognition of minority business icons, which became the foundation of BMA's legacy. Over the years, BMA had distinguished itself as a professional marketing association, which addressed the needs of corporate employees and show-cased the accomplishments of minority businesses.

BMA's tenth president, James L. Roberts, broke new ground by strengthening BMA's educational component. Roberts became an attractive candidate for president of BMA before assuming the presidency when he wrote a letter to the editor of <u>The Baltimore Sun Newspaper,</u> January 26th, 1980 that reads:

Sir, I was greatly appalled when I read that the Commissioner of Higher Education, Sheldon Knorr, had implied in his memo to the State Board of Higher Education that he questioned the quality of education of students who graduate from Morgan State University. I feel that no one is better qualified to evaluate the quality of students that Morgan State University is graduating than the numerous major corporations and government agencies that hire Morgan graduates, as well as the professional schools that admit them. It should be pointed out that Morgan State University has more college, graduate and professional school recruiters than any school in the State of Maryland in proportion to student enrollment. Morgan State University has averaged more than 300 recruiters a year over the past five years. During the 1978-79 school year, Morgan State had 305 corporate and government recruiters that selected on campus and 97 graduate or professional school recruiters looking to attract Morgan graduates to their institution..."

In 1984, Roberts, Director of the Center for Career Placement at Morgan State University, became BMA's "education president," who presented as his platform, several educational initiatives that served as the foundation for others to follow.

Since in 1977, Roberts hosted the popular weekly radio program: Career Focus, on WEAA, 88.9 FM Radio Station. Roberts focused his attention on the "Changing Job Markets," bringing to the studio audience major industry leaders who shared employment trends that were useful to both young college graduates and seasoned professionals seeking new career opportunities.

Pictured above, Roberts interacts with students at Southwestern Senior High School.

The premier effort that Roberts initiated was the creation of The Incentive Connection (TIC) program. It was designed as an educational mentoring program that initially provided Southwestern, Frederick Douglass and Lake Clifton high schools educational guidance and career counselling. Students in these selected schools were paired with mentors in professions of their interests. Mentoring sessions, mock interviews, résumé writing, job search skills, and tutoring were carried out in the classrooms and on the premises of participating businesses. When asked about the success of the TIC program at a lecture seminar, Roberts reported that the TIC program is succeeding because it is giving the students in the program a "leg-up" on the competition by providing them with useful skills to obtain employment and admission to college.

Roberts further asserted that *"For some students, the mentoring program provided them with a level playing field that would enhance the student's marketability, and at the same time, handed to the students a set of tools necessary to compete on any front."* His efforts did not stop at the high school and college levels. He was on a mission to expose elementary school students to the world of work, and as a result of his zeal and foresightedness, he encouraged the BMA membership to adopt Westside Elementary School. Members of BMA mentored students and assisted the principal and teachers with educational resources, which were limited due to tight school budgets.

As Roberts was busy shaping BMA's educational programs, Samuel T. Daniels, Executive Director of the Baltimore Council for Equal Business Opportunity (CEBO), was looking back over the past eighteen years with pride as he and other business leaders in Baltimore brought CEBO to the city of Baltimore. This organization provided specialized assistance to minority businesses, a concept borne out of the National Commission on Civil Disorders in 1966. CEBO provided services, including business development, technical management, and financial assistance.

Daniels orchestrated minority participation in Baltimore city construction projects, development of minority business goals for Baltimore's Harbor Place, and a model minority business enterprise program for the state highway system. The leadership Daniels provided in the African American community was so impressive that he, by unanimous acclamation, became BMA's sixteenth Business Award Honoree.

Dorothy Brunson, President and Chief Executive Officer of WEBB Radio Station, had carved-out a niche for herself in the radio communication industry. Brunson started her career in 1960 in the print communications industry. By 1964, she had joined the broadcast side of communications industry, and by 1969, was the assistant general manager of a radio station, WWRL, New York City. At the time of her award, Brunson owned WEBB Radio in Baltimore, Maryland, WIGO in Atlanta, Georgia, and WBMS Radio in Wilmington, North Carolina. Her awards for communications excellence and for being a "fighter" for the rights of people were extensive. They included: The National Conference of Christians and Jews, Black citizens for a Fair Media, and The National Association of Media Women. Her talents as a shrewd businessperson did not go unnoticed in Baltimore or elsewhere in the country. Brunson was regularly sought after for speaking engagements and television appearances. BMA was no exception to the growing interest in Brunson, and it seized the opportunity to have her become its seventeenth Business Awards recipient.

Calvin Anderson, BMA's eleventh president, saw the benefits of the educational programs that were developed by James Roberts.

Pictured , Calvin Anderson, BMA members, Westside Elem. staff, at Career Day

He collaborated extensively with Roberts to capture the essence of the programs, which were operated by BMA.

Anderson was an administrator with the Social Security Administration. He was trained in systems analyses and fine-tuned BMA's educational programs as he proudly "carried the banner" that permanently etched the educational initiatives in the forefront of BMA's programs. In his greetings at the Business Awards Dinner banquet, Anderson acknowledged the business relations between the Baltimore Sun newspaper. He emphasized the important alliance with Career Day and the Incentive Connection of BMA.

In 1986, Osborne A. Payne, President of Broadway - Payne, Inc., received BMA's eighteenth Business Award. Payne was a distinguished educator from Virginia who served as an advisor to the U.S. Government in Liberia, West Africa. He brought to Baltimore years of experience as an administrator and early on seized lucrative business opportunities. He first established his McDonald's franchise in 1975 and was one of the first McDonald's owner-operators in the country to receive a McDonald's Golden Arch Award for excellence in operations. Payne also operated Baltimore Specialty Tours, a business with a unique twist in recreational planning that specialized in limousine and yacht services. Payne served on national and local boards and was regularly sought after by fledgling businesses for advice and his proven ability to get the job done. His proven ability won him praise and honors from many organizations in Baltimore city.

Attending the dinner are L-R Joseph Haskins, James McLean, Art Petersen, Tom Carey and Nate Chapman.

Pictured at the Awards Dinner are William Anderson, Angela Davis, and the honoree, Osborne B. Payne.

As with any organization, a minority of BMA members accomplished the lion's share of the work. Naturally, any imbalance in work among the members was bound to cause discussions as to why things were that way. In the later part of 1986, these discussions grew rather intense. The Board of Directors met and decided that the organization was not replacing talent lost to corporate moves. The plain facts were that BMA was losing valuable members and it had not groomed others to step-up and take leadership positions. New members were again tapped to hold key leadership positions, and of course, it was risky using unproven talent to assume important positions; either way the options were limited.

"What the organization needs is a vision for the future!" shouted Ackneil Muldrow during a heated discussion at one of the meetings. Muldrow continued, *"Any organization that has not carefully charted its future is doomed to fail."* Those statements were enough for the membership to "close the deal" on its leader of the future, thus Muldrow was selected for an unprecedented third term as president of BMA.

Under his new leadership, Muldrow carefully integrated new ideas from the younger members with proven programs and activities of the past. This strategy worked, and according to Chairman of the Board, Calvin Anderson, *"BMA was off again, continuing its good works that have brought us this far."* Community services continued with the Afro's Santa, Blue Chip-In, and The Incentive Connection. BMA also expanded its charity giving to the United Negro College Fund and sponsored the Adopt-A-School program, for which BMA provided school supplies and speakers for the selected elementary schools.

Arthur W. Lambert, Owner & Operator of Lambert Insurance Agency, Inc. was BMA's nineteenth Business Awards honoree.

Lambert, owner-operator of Lambert's Insurance Agency, founded this independent insurance agency. Lambert began his career as an insurance agent with Continental Insurance Companies in New Jersey in 1958, and in 1964, he joined the International Harvester organization as an industrial management trainee. During his tenure with Continental, he was placed in charge of training new adjusters and was selected to conduct a special project in marketing research.

Lambert worked hard at his new job and even worked harder operating his own business at night until he had secured sufficient resources to make the transition as the full-time owner-operator of Lambert Insurance agency. There were numerous trade associations to which Lambert belonged along with active civic responsibilities. He received a Bachelor of Arts Degree in Mathematics and Economics from Hobart College in Geneva New York. Academic achievements came easy for Lambert, to include being on the Dean's list and serving as president of honor societies during his sophomore and junior years. He was active in sports and played on Hobart's basketball and football teams for four years.

In his junior and senior years, Lambert was voted as the most valuable player of the football team and was also the captain of the basketball team. He held memberships on boards of Independent Insurance Agents of Metropolitan Baltimore, Inc., Independent Agents of Maryland, Inc., and President of the Council of Equal Business Opportunity (CEBO), Inc. in Baltimore. Lambert was a long-time member and served proudly as Basilus of Omega Psi Phi Fraternity, Incorporation, Pi Omega Chapter.

In 1988, William March became BMA's twentieth Business Award honoree. March was the founder of one of the largest African American-owned funeral service companies in the country. He got the idea to become an undertaker from a man whom he met in the pool hall and launched the family-owned funeral home in 1957. From the living room of his row house at 928 East North Avenue in Baltimore, March worked as an apprentice without a salary at Halstead Funeral Home and later became a partner in the funeral home.

While working at the U.S. Postal Service and Halstead, March founded his own funeral home, which functioned at the time of his award as his business office. In the beginning of the fledging enterprise, the majority of his clients were veterans and welfare cases, which eventually earned him the reputation as the "welfare undertaker."

In 1973, March founded the King Memorial Park Cemetery of 154 acres in Baltimore County. Building his enterprise was not easy. Even as his business grew steadily in the 1970s, March had difficulty persuading loan officers to advance him money. He believed that he was rejected because of his race. Financing for his East Baltimore funeral home came from the

Small Business Administration, an African American Savings and Loan association, and $150,000 of his own money.

By 1978, March constructed a sprawling funeral home in the 100 block of East North Avenue. Seven years later, he built a second facility in West Baltimore in the 4300 block of Wabash Avenue. He was an ardent supporter of community projects and charitable organizations; he generously designated part of his profits to go back to the community. Through the Thelma March Scholarship Fund, a memorial to his sister, March granted scholarships to students attending Dunbar and Douglass high schools. March became an enormous success in Baltimore; nonetheless his business pursuits never overshadowed his benevolence.

Knowing first-hand the importance of access to capital for small business development, March helped to finance and co-found the Harbor Bank of Maryland, the city's first minority-owned commercial bank. He also helped to restore the Orchard Street Church, a landmark that sheltered slaves as they made their way to freedom along the Underground Railroad.

The big question in 1989 was *what do BMA and the Market Center Development Corporation (MCDC) have in common?*

The obvious answer was David K. Elam Sr., an administrator of MCDC. Elam became BMA's thirteenth president whose educational background and work experiences made him a unique choice for the job. Known for his deal-making skills, working with public and private organizations, and planning commercial and residential developments, Elam saw the advantages of forging partnerships. He had a strong entrepreneurial spirit coupled with a quiet but shrewd management style. In a nutshell, Elam was a man of action; he knew how to get the job done, but most importantly, he was the stabilizing influence among the membership. In his acceptance speech, Elam challenged the membership to *"Go forward in the years ahead and exact from yourself, your very best and never waiver from the goals because it is your steadfastness and dedication to the principles, that will take a mere germ of an idea and transform it into nodes of energy, capable of growing in geometric proportions."*

It was the influence of Elam's commitment to strong principles that attracted BMA to Norwood "Ted" Coates, who built Century 21 Associated Real Estate, Inc. His real estate company rose to prominence in the Baltimore metropolitan area during the early to mid-1980s.

Coates built his business through hard work and his hands-on approach to management. His personable character, despite his success, never caused him to lose his common touch.

In 1990, Williams L. "Little Willie" Adams became BMA's twenty-second Business Award's recipient. Adams was an able real estate businessman whose name was synonymous with assistance to African American businesses in Baltimore.

When Baltimore was a segregated town, Adams helped to open doors for thousands who had been locked out of the system. His business interest created jobs, housing, entertainment, and minority business development. Although never a candidate for public office, Adams' support of African American candidates was legendary; his political savvy was enviable.

In the six decades of his career, he was among the first African Americans to forge political alliances that cut across racial lines. Adams' impact on West Baltimore's politics was dramatically clear and impressive.

The legendary Adams left an indelible mark on the landscape of Baltimore; his legacy was historic and worthy of high praise. He won "big" in business and politics against almost insurmountable odds. In the 1950s, Adams owned Carr's Beach in Annapolis, a black amusement park. He and Theo Rogers owned A&R Development, a major development company on the east coast.

Adams, pictured above was an avid golfer. (Special Collections, University of Maryland Libraries).

Working against the odds, Ovetta M. Moore became the fourteenth president and the third women to hold that position in BMA's history in September1991.

Ovetta Moore sought and won the presidency with zeal and determination. She possessed a no-nonsense style of leadership and pulled together a core of BMA members who shared her philosophy of being direct and forthright with a win-win attitude.

Despite a substantial downturn in the economy, corporate downsizing, and in the face of several BMA members and supporters being between jobs, Moore nonetheless was set on rebuilding the infrastructure of BMA to ensure accountability of its programs to its clients. She also used all resources available to her while generating considerable interest among other women in BMA to assume leadership positions traditionally held by men.

Moore expanded the educational programs of TIC, supported the College Bound program, and obtained from the Internal Revenue Service (IRS), the long sought-after designation of BMA as a 501(C)(3) tax exempt organization. The significance of this designation was that BMA was recognized for the first time as a charitable organization whose mission was primarily educational. As a result, BMA then had an obligation to design and carry forward its programs that substantially focused on the delivery of services that impacted educational issues. Moore took this new designation as a license for BMA's Educational Committee to run full throttle with BMA's educational programs. Upon first learning of its tax-exempt status, Moore said, *"We now have an obligation to ourselves and our corporate supporters to carry forward the educational torch of BMA in name and in deed."*

BMA's twenty-third Business Award Banquet's theme in 1991, "African American Women Networking in the 90s," set the tone for the selection of Sina McGimpsey Reid, whose entrepreneurial savvy made a major impact on area food chains.

"Dogs Plus," the trade name of Sina McGimpsey Reid's business, had locations in Owings Mills' mall, Harbor Place, and Union Station in Washington, D.C. She was also the Executive

Vice President of Broadway-Payne franchises. She contributed her time freely to charitable organizations and was the Chair of the Board of Directors for the Associated Black Charities, an organization to which she was genuinely committed (*Archives of The Baltimore Marketing Association, Inc., Program Booklet, Twenty-Third Annual Business Award Dinner, December 6, 1991*).

Rounding out its twenty-five years of service in 1992, BMA selected as its twenty-fourth honoree, George L. Russell, Jr., "a man for all seasons." Russell had a wealth of talents in law and business and politics. He is currently partner with the law firm, Piper and Marbury. Russell made a name for himself as a tough, hard-nosed, smart attorney who established the first major African American law firm in the city of Baltimore. He also served for a while as judge of the Circuit Court of Baltimore City. Russell was the driving force and first Chairman of the Board of the Harbor Bank of Maryland, the first African American bank in the State of Maryland.

The list of firsts for Russell is extensive. He became a prominent figure as a major influence over policy decisions in government and business throughout the State of Maryland (*Archives of The Baltimore Marketing Association, Inc., Program Booklet, Twenty-Fourth Annual Business Award Dinner, December 3, 1992*).

In September 1993, Kenneth N. Oliver was elected President of BMA. With a B.S Degree in Business from the University of Baltimore and an MBA from Morgan State University, Oliver became a "Dollar$ and Sense" executive. Oliver immediately set as his first-year goal the financial and operational accountability of BMA. Through Oliver's efforts, BMA continued its community service with the United Negro College Fund, The Academy of Finance, Baltimore City Public Schools, Adopt-A-School (Dr. Roland Patterson Sr.'s Academy), Associated Black Charities and the College Bound program.

Oliver's administration established the Harold D. Young, Esquire, Leadership Award, and Young became the first recipient of the award.

Oliver was named the second recipient of the Harold D. Young, Esquire Leadership Award. Oliver exhibited a keen interest and knowledge of the needs of the Maryland small business sector and through his efforts as then Senior Vice President of Marketing of the Development Credit Fund (DCF), he was committed to helping owners of small businesses realize their financial aspirations.

After joining the DCF, Oliver helped to guide the firm to fund more than $25 million dollars in loans to small businesses. He also helped the company obtain funding from the city of Baltimore, which led to managing the Community Development Block Grant Loan Fund and later the Empowerment Zone Loan Fund. He took the lead in establishing a successful pilot program that helped establish a minority-owned athletic specialty retail store in Maryland, Washington, Washington DC, Northern Virginia, and Delaware.

Oliver joined BMA in 1983 and held positions of Treasurer, Executive Vice President, Chairman of the Board, and Director at Large. Under his administration as President, he was applauded for his efforts to include the broader corporate community in BMAs activities and programs. He was a member of the Baltimore County Planning Board where he served as Co-Chair of the Capital Budget Committee and Vice Chairman of the Board. He later was elected to the Baltimore County Council, representing the northwest district of the county.

Upon graduating from the University of Baltimore in 1973, Oliver joined the Equitable Bank as a management trainee. Within six months, he was assigned to the Pikesville Branch as Assistant Manager. In 1974, he was assigned to the Reisterstown Road Plaza Branch, and shortly thereafter, was promoted to Branch Manager of the Liberty Road Office with expanded responsibilities in marketing, investment management, and supervision. In 1980, Oliver received yet another promotion to the Woodlawn Office, where he significantly increased bank revenues by increasing business contacts with businesses and civic organizations.

He joined the faculty of Coppin State College and the American Institute of Banking. Oliver received a Master's degree in Business Administration with a concentration in Finance, which made him an attractive candidate to numerous organizations, which included the Investing in Baltimore Committee, the Hannah Moore School, Liberty/Randallstown Coalition, MD/DC Minority Supplier Development Council, Park Heights Development Corporation Revolving Loan Fund, Northwest Baltimore Corporation, The Robert Morris Associates, Maryland

Bankers Association, National Association of Credit Managers, Glove Tilman Learning Center, and a founding member of Urban Bankers Association.

Governor Harry Hughes appointed Oliver to the Advisory Board of the Walter P. Carter Mental Retardation Center. County Executive Donald P. Hutchins appointed him to the Private Industry Council and Oliver was appointed to the Baltimore County Human Relations Commission, and County Executive Parris Glendenning appointed him to the Prince George's County Bankers Task Force (*Archives of The Baltimore Marketing Association, Inc.*).

In 1993, impressed with Harlow Fullwood Jr.'s (1941-2007) business acumen and civic and community accomplishments, Oliver named Fullwood the twenty-fifth Business Award recipient. He was a well-respected business, family man, a decorated former policeman, and a native of Asheville, North Carolina. He graduated from the Community College of Baltimore and Virginia Union University. He was married to the former Elnora Bassett, with whom he raised two children, Paquita Fullwood Stokes and Harlow Fullwood III.

Harlow Fulllwood made Baltimore his home for several years and served the city of Baltimore and state of Maryland diligently and enthusiastically throughout his business, professional, and civic endeavors. His many accomplishments and awards in the business community included the acquisition of several Kentucky Fried Chicken franchises, and he became the first black American in history commended for leading the entire state in KFC gross sales. He was honored by *The Baltimore Sun Newspaper* as one of fifty leading black businesses in Maryland. He also received the Governor's Recognition Award for Growth and Development as one of five successful small and minority businesses in the state. Harlow Fullwood was cited at the national level for his entrepreneurial achievements and was honored with the Austin, Texas Metropolitan Business Resource Center National Minority Franchisee of the Year Award (AMBRC), and in 1992, he received the National Blue Chip Enterprise Award presented by the Connecticut Mutual Life Insurance Company, the U.S. Chamber of Commerce, and Nation's Business.

Fullwood was devoted to civic performance and generously facilitated the achievement of positive relations between people of the local and global community. These efforts were noted by his establishment, the Fullwood Foundation, Inc., which provided support in volunteer services and/or cash grants to the community. He was so dedicated to the progress and achievements of black colleges that he was inducted into the 1990 National Black Alumni Hall of Fame in Atlanta, Georgia. Other awards that Fullwood received were the Distinguished Service Award presented by the Baltimore City Police Department, 1979 Policeman of the Year, Evening Sun Newspapers in 1992, Who's Who Among Black Americans in 1990, and was inducted into the Central Intercollegiate Athletic Association Hall of Fame with a Jimmy Swartz Medallion, which was presented by former Governor, Millard Tawes. He called Fullwood a natural born achiever, an organizer, and a leader. As for Fullwood, he described his success in a quote from George Washington Carver by stating, *"How far you go in life depends upon your being tender with the young, compassionate with the aged, sympathetic with the striving and tolerant of both the weak and the strong, because sometime in your life you will have been one, or all of these"* (*Archives of The Baltimore Marketing Association, Inc., Program Booklet, Twenty-Fifth Annual Business Award Dinner, December 2, 1993*).

HAROLD D. YOUNG, ESQUIRE LEADERSHIP AWARD

In 1993, BMA Board of Directors passed a resolution creating the Harold D. Young Esquire Leadership Award. The first recipient of the award was Harold D. Young, the person after whom the award was named. This award was presented to a BMA member who provided the organization with strong, steady, and imaginative leadership, demonstrated BMA dedication above and beyond the call of duty, and helped advance the goals of the organization through total loyalty to the total organization.

Young had distinguished himself as a family man, legal counsel, government official, civic leader, community servant, and business advisor. At the U.S. Department of Housing and Urban Development, Young worked closely with mayors, county executives, and town mangers on significant issues in housing, planning, and economic development. He published or presented several papers, was guest lecturer at Morgan State University, and had extensive speaking engagements in the State and throughout the country.

Young was involved in a number of community and service organizations, such as the President of The Northwest Little League, the former Baltimore City Committee of the Maryland State Commission on Afro-American History and Culture, the Big Brothers of Baltimore City, and Providence Baptist Church. He joined BMA in 1970 and was BMA's president for five years (1976-1980). During his tenure, he initiated the John S. Sheppard Jr.'s Scholarship Fund, Black Business Hall of Fame, supported efforts for the formation of the Maryland State Office of Minority Business Enterprise, BMA's legal counsel, and the Business Compendium, a quarterly newsletter (*Archives of The Baltimore Marketing Association, Inc.*).

Allen Quille was named the recipient of the H.G. Parks Jr. Award at BMA's twenty-sixth Business Awards Dinner in 1994.

Long before the Inner Harbor became a trendy marketplace and tourist attraction, Baltimore's port bustled with shipping enterprises and hundreds of businesses supporting that trade.

It was during this time, more than sixty years prior, that an illustrious career of one of our city's leading entrepreneurs and philanthropist was born. Quille went from quiet obscurity to one who is synonymous with a big city magnet.

Quille's parking had evolved into two separate ventures – a joint venture with Crown Parking that provided parking east coast facilities in cities of New York, Pennsylvania, Baltimore, Annapolis, and Washing D.C. The other venture was Quille Parking with numerous parking lots throughout Baltimore city. He was also owner of several service stations in Baltimore. Quille had established a reputation as a committed humanitarian of causes that crossed ethnic, racial, and geographic lines. Respected by heads of state and the common man alike. He held the admiration of business colleagues, competitors, the hearts of children of East Baltimore as well as East Jerusalem.

Comments made about Quille were that *"He just loves people – He's concerned about people – What touched his heart was the condition under which we were living, especially after working with children all day."*

Quille was born to a family of modest means, spending his earliest years on Gilmore Street. Quille's father, Allen Quille Sr., sought a better life for his eight-year-old son and sent him to live with the Reverend John Curtis in Calvert County in Southern Maryland until his teen years when he returned to Baltimore and landed a job as a parking lot attendant. Recipients of Quille's generosity included Boy Scouts and Girl Scouts of America, United Negro College

Fund, Liberty Medical Center, Coppin State College, the American Israel Society, Safety First Club of Maryland and Mississippi NAACP (*Archives of The Baltimore Marketing Association, Inc., Program Booklet, Twenty-Sixth Annual Business Award Dinner, December 1, 1994*).

The Baltimore Marketing Association had been an important part of Sherry Reed's life for eight years prior to receiving the Harold D. Young Esquire Leadership Award. Reed worked on several committees, including the Annual Awards dinner, the Annual Spring Ball, Membership Committee, Education Committee, Adopt-A-School (Career Day), and the Entertainment Committee. She also would serve as Assistant Secretary, Executive Secretary, Co-Chairperson Annual Awards Dinner, and a member of the Board of Directors. Reed graduated from the Community College of Baltimore and the University of Baltimore.

By 1994, Reed had already accrued twenty-eight years at Williams & Wilkins Company, Waverly, Inc., a publisher of medical books and journals. She worked in the Advertising Sales Department, Journal Division of Waverly. Positions she held included sales and marketing of numerous publications in nephrology, radiology, gastroenterology, transportation, colon and rectum surgery, and rheumatology. She was the Regional Sales Representative responsible for advertising sales for more than twenty-five publications. Prior to working in the Journal Division of Waverly, she was a member of the Book Division for over nineteen years. As an Educational Sales Representative, Reed enjoyed traveling throughout the country promoting books to medical, dental, and allied health professional schools. During 1980 to1981, Reed received the Highest Sales Award, and in 1981 to 1982, she received the Educational Representative of the Year Award.

Reed was a member of the Walters Art Gallery, where she served as Intern Docent. She enjoyed conducting tours for adults and students, especially for the African Zion and the Secrecy Exhibits. Other affiliations included NAACP where she served as the Fundraising Committee, member of the Mayor's Council on Women in Business, Pharmaceutical Advertising Council, and member of the Healthcare Business Association.

In December 1995, BMA selected Joseph Haskins Jr., Chair, President, and CEO of the Harbor Bank of Maryland, its second banker, as the recipient of its twenty-seventh H.G. Parks Jr. Business Award. Haskins' banking career led him from Chase Manhattan Bank in New York, First Union in New Jersey, back to Baltimore as Coppin State College's Vice President for Business and Finance and then to Prudential Securities as a Portfolio Investment Manager. After attaining a B.A. in Economics from Morgan State University, Haskins went on to successfully receiving his M.B.A. in Finance from New York University and a Master's of Liberal Arts in Economics from Johns Hopkins University.

Haskins, one of the founders of Harbor Bank, opened its doors in September 1982 with $2.1 million in assets, becoming the first minority owned full-service commercial bank in Baltimore's history. Of the twenty-one initial board members, there were five different nationalities and two women (*Archives of The Baltimore Marketing Association, Inc., Program Booklet, Twenty-Seventh Annual Business Award Dinner, December 7th, 1995*).

Gerald Williams was elected President and CEO of BMA in 1996 where he touted $80,000 in cumulative scholarship awards.

Williams' passion as BMA's president was to stimulate involvement in community service: United Negro College Fund, the Academy of Finance in Baltimore City Public Schools, Adopt-A-School, Associated Black Charities and College Bound.

Pictured is Greenspring Middle School adopted by BMA in 1996.

Williams and his cabinet sought and received acceptance from Cathy L. Hughes, who was named in December 1996 the twenty-eighth Henry G. Parks Jr. Awards Honoree.

Cathy Hughes was owner and CEO of Radio One Company. Hughes and company operated seven radio stations in the Baltimore/Washington Corridor and in Atlanta, Georgia. A native of Omaha, Nebraska, Hughes was a pioneer in the broadcast industry long before she purchased her first station. She became interested in radio while attending Creighton University where she worked with the campus-owned station. Hughes was an investor in KOWH, a black-owned radio station in Omaha. After sixty to seventy hours a week with her investment, she knew radio inside and out and had worked every job at the station.

In 1971, Hughes moved to Washington, D.C. and lectured at Howard University School of Communication under the direction of Tony Brown. She was instrumental in helping to create a curriculum that would be accredited by academic associations around the world. In 1975, she served as the Vice President and General Manager of WHUR-FM at Howard University. As the first female general manager, Hughes created the most successful, nationally-used night-time format, "The Quiet Storm," and increased advertisement revenues from $300,000 to $3.5 million.

Seeing the growing need of the African American community for a view and a voice, Hughes purchased WOL-AM in 1980 and created a slogan "Where Knowledge is Power." The Cathy Hughes Show debut was a year later and became the constant source of information and empowerment to its community-based listeners.

Hughes also purchased WKYS-FM, the powerhouse at 93.9 FM from Albimar Communications, Inc., which was a $34 million deal, at the time was the largest radio transaction between two minority owned companies. Hughes' son, Alfred Liggins, served as Radio One's President and General Manager.

Hughes was awarded an honorary doctorate from Sojourner-Douglas College and Turner Broadcasting, a coveted Trumpet Award honoring African Americans' achievements. In fulfilling her dream to economically empower African Americans, Radio One boasted a staff of over 300 employees, of whom 95% were African Americans.

Hughes often stated, "I tell young sisters to keep their eye on the prize and accept the fact that racism and sexism are the realities of a black woman's existence. I don't attempt to change the world of radio, I attempt to create my own world where racism and sexism do not prevail and to do that, you must be the owner" (*Archives of The Baltimore Marketing Association, Inc., Twenty-Eighth Annual Business Award Dinner, December 5th, 1996*).

In 1997, BMA benefited from broad community support from Mayor L. Kurt Smoke and a renewed and long-term commitment from WJZ-TV Radio Station who co-sponsored the Awards Dinner.

At the 1997 Awards Dinner, James E. Johnson, BMA's President & CEO, spoke proudly of the benefits of the organization's accomplishments and singled-out educational development programs and efforts made to promote minority entrepreneurial opportunities during his administration. Johnson was a tireless worker, holding several positions in BMA, and in 1995 was the recipient of the Harold D. Young Esquire, Leadership Award (*Archives of The Baltimore Marketing Association, Inc.*).

The keynote speaker for the Awards Dinner was Kelvin E. Boston, a former director of the Calvert New Africa Mutual Fund and CEO of Boston Media, Inc., the multimedia company that produced the "Smart Money Moves" television series. Henry T. Baines Sr. won the support of BMA members to become the twenty-ninth recipient of the H.G. Parks Jr. Business Award. Baines migrated from Wilson, North Carolina to Baltimore City with his wife and children in 1962. He was an outstanding student and learned the meaning of "work ethic" at a young age from his mother. His progressive career in the grocery industry began as a grocery clerk to save money for a college education. After three months, Baines' hard work and commitment was recognized by senior management. Within four years, after numerous promotions, he became store manager.

In 1978, Baines opened his first store in the Park Heights community of Northwest Baltimore, the Super Thrift, comprised of family members and friends. Later in 1981, Baines merged with Edward Hunt, creating Stop, Shop, and Save Corporation. Operating his stores in the city of Baltimore, he served the very communities other businesses chose to alienate. Baines' motto and secret of success is "Treat people fairly." The corporation had fifteen stores with annual sales in excess of $108 million. Under Baines's leadership, the Stop, Shop, and Save Corporation was at the time the largest minority-owned grocery chain in the nation.

Baines, The Innovator, as described by many of his colleagues, strove for the "quality business." He defined his strategy as one which creates a business atmosphere that is a conduit for growth and provides a positive, productive, and prosperous work environment for his employees. Baines was an incubator for several start-up businesses and provided opportunities and resources to aspiring entrepreneurs (*Archives of The Baltimore Marketing Association, Inc., Program Booklet, Twenty-Ninth Annual Business Award Dinner, December 4, 1997*).

As President and CEO of BMA, Denise A. Smith worked with the broader Baltimore business community in 1998 in continuing BMA's brand of professionalism, student support, and outreach programs and recognition of Baltimore's outstanding business leaders.

Denise Alexander Smith embodied the spirit, commitment, and energy exemplified and was in 1996 named recipient of the Harold D. Young Esquire Leadership Award. At the time of the award, Smith was a BMA Board member and spent countless hours with the Adopt-A-School program by providing financial support and other resources to the Greenspring Middle School.

She worked as an Advertising Account Manager for WOPC-FM, Baltimore's #1 Country Music Station. She received a B.S. degree in Business Administration from Morgan State University. Smith enjoyed early success in the insurance industry where she worked at the Hartford Steam Boiler Inspection and Insurance Company and the Chubb Group Insurance Company. She also worked as an Account Representative for Directory Advertising with Southwestern Bell.

Smith's professional affiliations include: Member, Board of Director, Upton Foundation, Advertising Association of Baltimore, Community Outreach Committee, Baltimore Symphony Orchestra, Volunteers of America, Chairperson, Morgan State University Gala XII, MSU Alumni Association, Lifetime Member, NAACP. Smith was recognized as an outstanding sales associate on numerous occasions, recipient of a Brother-to-Brother award for mentoring and her volunteerism, an award recipient from Brown Memorial Church for volunteering for the Homeless Shelter.

Pictured below: BMA members salute Denise Smith and James Johnson for their outstanding leadership in BMA.

Smith's organizational efforts culminated with her selecting as honorary chairperson, a panel of distinguished community and business leaders who were showcased at thirtieth Annual Business Awards Dinner. 4th District City Councilwoman Sheila Dixon, Marcellus W. Alexander, Jr, WJZ-TV, Daniel P. Henson, II, Baltimore City Director and Commissioner of Housing, Robert F. Dashiell, Esquire, Keith Adams, Pless Jones, P & J Contractors, Robert Clay Company, Gerard Brice and Denny Brice, D & G Contractors, K & K Trucking, Inc., and George Mahoney, Monumental Paving & Excavating, Inc.

Smith's efforts led to the naming of Randolph Phipps as the recipient of the Henry G. Parks, Jr. Award.

Rudolph Phipps was born and raised in rural Virginia. He grew to become an ambitious entrepreneur and gained substantial experience in the construction industry. This earned him a position as superintendent with a construction firm. Phipps was impatient with working for other companies and wanted more.

In 1993, he established his own firm, the Phipps Construction Contracting, Inc. Phipps was a strong proponent for hard work and used his experience, skills, and outgoing personality to work on major development and construction projects for Baltimore city and large construction development firms.

Phipps' repertoire of construction tasks was vast and included: land cleaning, demolition, site grading, storm drainage, sanitary sewer and water projects, paving masonry, fencing, blacktopping, and excavation. Phipps operated a fleet of dump trucks, earthmoving and demolition equipment (*Archives of The Baltimore Marketing Association, Inc., Program Booklet, Thirtieth Annual Business Awards Dinner, December 3rd, 1998*).

———————

Advancing the goals of the Baltimore Marketing Association through personal loyalty, work, and leadership were qualities that led BMA to name Doretha M. Huntley as the recipient of the Harold D. Young Esquire Leadership Award in 1998.

Huntley served as Vice President of Finance, Executive Secretary and Board of Directors.

Doretha Huntley was a native of the Eastern Shore and attended Wor-Wic College and Salisbury State University where she received a degree in accounting in 1978. Upon graduation she was employed as the first African American female at Milford W. Tilley, Inc., a construction, contracting, and real estate company. Huntley assumed a position in 1980 with the American Credit Indemnity Corporation, a subsidiary of Commercial Credit Corporation. Huntley serviced and maintained credit information on many Fortune 500 corporations and quickly rose to the rank as Senior Rate Analyst and later worked in the Risk Management Division.

In 1985, Huntley was recruited and encouraged to assume the position of supervisor with the Tax Accounting department for the state of Maryland, Comptroller of the Treasury. In her latest position, she was responsible for the recovery of assets and the auditing of tax records filed by corporations seeking bankruptcy protection.

Because of her love for children and the elderly, Huntley spent her spare time volunteering with the Baltimore County Public Schools (*Archives of The Baltimore Marketing Association, Inc.*).

 In 1999, Oliver and his administration selected as the Thirty-First H. G. Parks, Jr. Award recipient, Eddie Carl Brown. He was the founder of Brown Capital Management and was known for his intelligence, passion, drive, and commitment. He completed high school at the age of sixteen and dreamed of being the first member of his family to attend college. After graduating from Howard University in 1961, Brown was hired by IBM as an electrical engineer and later earned a Master's of Science degree in Electrical Engineering and followed by a Master's of Business Administration.

In 1973, Brown was hired by T. Rowe Price where he rose to the position of Vice President. Albeit, having had a successful career at T. Rowe Price, Brown's drive and passion led him to establish Brown Capital Management, Inc., where he managed a portfolio of $5.1 billion dollars. In 1994, he and his wife, Sylvia (supported by his daughters, Tonya and Jennifer), created the Eddie C. and Sylvia Brown Foundation. This foundation was established to assist African American children in Baltimore (*Archives of The Baltimore Marketing Association, Inc., Program Booklet, Thirty-First Annual Business Awards Dinner, December 2, 1999*).

Another highlight of 1999 was BMA's involvement with the Roland Patterson Sr. Academy School (Middle School) during Career Day activities.

Photograph by John h. Murphy, III.

Several members of the business community were involved: Bessie Weaver, V.P. of Education, BBM and Associates, Kenneth Oliver of BMA and Development Credit Fund, Michael Cassell of Creative Realty, Sherry L. Reed of Lippincott Williams & Wilkins, Benjamin Lewis, Abrams, Foster, Nole & Williams, Larry Smith, CEO, Council of Equal Business Opportunity, Jeff Smithery, DHMH, Michael Easterling, The Chapman Company, Monique Knight, Arthur Anderson, Sarah Crockett and Richard Van Dyke of Drugnet. Principal Gerry W. Mansfield and students welcomed BMA to Career Day, so each participant was exposed to successful professionals with whom they were able to rub shoulders for a day. Years later Principal Mansfield and students remained as an integral part of BMA's educational outreach efforts (*Archives of The Baltimore Marketing Association, Inc.*).

On December 7th, 2000, Oliver and a select committee unanimously agreed that Ackneil M. Muldrow, II, would be named the thirty-second recipient of the Henry G. Parks, Jr. Business Award. If having served as president of BMA for an unprecedented third-term was not spectacular enough, Muldrow's accomplishments in the business community were unparalleled. Not to mention, just twelve months earlier in December 1999, Muldrow was named recipient of the Harold D. Young Esquire Leadership Award for the strength of his character, breadth of his leadership, and his demand for excellence. He was appointed to the prestigious position as a gubernatorial appointee as Commissioner of the Maryland State Lottery Commission (1972-1975) and had his own business, BMA Insurance Agency, Inc. (1974-1976). He was a highly sought-after insightful member of numerous boards of directors of major businesses (for profit and charitable, educational, and medical corporations) in the Metropolitan Baltimore Area.

Muldrow's broad civic interests allowed him to serve as a Director of the publicly – traded Waverly, Inc., later renamed, Lippincott Williams & Wilkins Co, a worldwide publisher of medical books and journals.

Clarice Carter, Steadman Graham, Keynote Speaker,
Honoree, Ackneil M. Muldrow, II and his wife, Ruth

Pictured are Denise Scott and Chazz Scott, Muldrow's daughter, grandson and wife.

Pictured with the honoree is, Ackneil M. Muldrow, III, son.

Mayor Kurt L. Schmoke, Muldrow, Board and staff celebrate
the grand opening of the Development Credit Fund.

Ackneil M. Muldrow, II
President & CEO

Lonnie Murray
Vice President, Finance

Kenneth N. Oliver
Vice President, Marketing

Natalie E. Braxton
Loan Administrator

Sharron P. Miller
Administrative Secretary

(Pictured left are employees who held key positions at DCF).

The crowning jewel of Muldrow's accomplishments was having been named President and CEO of the Development Credit Fund (DCF). Muldrow realized at DCF that his life had come full circle – from him wanting to gain "access" to equal opportunity at the lunch counter in Greensboro, North Carolina to numerous letters he had written to mayors of Baltimore City urging them to grant black businesses equal access to capital for contracting opportunities.

With his appointment as President and CEO of DCF, Muldrow had uniquely positioned himself to make capital accessible to small and minority-owned businesses. DCF was a $12 million commercial loan fund that made loans to small and minority-owned businesses in the Mid-Atlantic region. DCF was formerly established in 1983 by six major commercial banks in Maryland. The initial revolving loan fund was funded at the level of $7.5 million.

DCF managed a $3 million Empowerment Zone revolving fund and $1.7 million Community Development Block Grant fund for Baltimore City's Department of Housing and Community Development.

Through a special partnership arrangement between NIKE Inc., the global athletic specialty-marketing firm, the Maryland Department of Business and Community Development, DCF was the administrator of a $1million loan fund.

DCF, through below-market financing, provided loans to traditionally disadvantaged businesses, working capital, new machinery, and modern equipment. DCF loans were also guaranteed by the U.S. Small Business and the Maryland Small Business Development Financing Authority Administration for loans between $5,000 to $750,000.

Thus, when the membership evaluated nominees for the thirty-second Henry G. Parks, Jr. Business Award, Muldrow won hands-down over other nominees. His broad community appeal drew a large crowd of supporters that included Raymond Haysbert, *HCR Consultants and Forum Caterers*, Samuel T. Daniels, *Prince Hall Grand Lodge*, Cathy Hughes, *Radio One*, John Seth, *Commercial Credit Company (Retired)*, Joy Bramble, *Baltimore Times*, Dr. Richard I. McKinney, *Past Grand Sire Archon*, Laurence Merlis, *Greater Baltimore Medical Center*, and Dr. Stephen C. Shimpff, *University of Maryland Medical Systems*.

Among other supporters of Muldrow at the Awards Banquet are Joseph Bryant, Sr. BMA member, State Delegate Adrienne Jones and Kenneth Oliver, President of BMA.

In the Baltimore Metropolitan area, small businesses were without adequate capital to maximize their businesses' bottom line. Local banks were unwilling to make less profitable loans, which left a void that was filled by the naming of Muldrow as President and CEO of the Development Credit Fund 1983.

Muldrow was also a member of the Board of Directors of the Baltimore Urban Coalition, the Baltimore City Cable Evaluation Board, Trustee Associate, Board of Trustees, College of Notre Dame of Maryland, member Chancellor's Advisory Board, University of Maryland System, Member Engineering Society Club of Baltimore, Northeast Regional Executive Officer, 45th Biennial Grand Boule, Sigma Pi Phi Fraternity and President of Lambda International Land Society, International Association in Land Economic development (*Archives of The Baltimore Marketing Association, Inc., Program Booklet, Thirty-Second Annual Business Awards dinner, December 7ᵗʰ, 2000).*

Lois A. McBride Esquire was the 2,000 recipient of the Harold D. Young Esquire Leadership Award. McBride was a nurse and an attorney. She was named partner at the prestigious Law Firm of Wright, Constable, & Skeen, L.L. P. McBride received her B.S.N. Degree from the University of Maryland School of Nursing and graduated with honors. Upon graduating from nursing school, McBride worked as a Pediatric Charge Nurse at the University of Maryland Hospital. She also worked as a Community Health Nurse for Carroll County. She later earned a M.S. Degree with a 4.0 GPA from the University of Maryland School of Nursing. McBride completed her J.D Degree at the University of Maryland School of Law in 1982 and practiced law with the Maryland Court of Appeals, United States District Court, and the Supreme Court of the United States.

Upon completion of her Master's Degree in Nursing, she taught as an Assistant Professor at the University of Maryland School of Nursing while attending law school full-time. She also taught at the University of Baltimore Law School, Morgan State University, and at the University of Maryland School of Nursing in Germany. McBride was a published author and consultant in the areas of health care and litigation. She joined the Baltimore Marketing Association in 1990 where she served as Counselor and Legal Consultant to the Board.

She was appointed to the Community College of Baltimore County Board, Maryland Bar Foundation, Fellow, Baltimore County Planning Board, and United Nations Conference, Istanbul and Turkey who appointed her as a health care legal consultant.

McBride was affiliated with numerous professional organizations, including the Baltimore City Bar Association as President, National Exchange Club, Baltimore County Bar Association, and the Chesapeake Nurse-Attorney. She was active in community service and was the recipient of numerous awards for her community and professional service *(Archives of The Baltimore Marketing Association, Inc.).*

Sherrie L. Reed was named President and CEO of BMA in 2001. Under her leadership, BMA had awarded over $100,000 in scholarships to students who attended area colleges and universities and to those organization, which had for the first time established the Ackneil M. Muldrow II Lifetime Achievement Award. Reed also focused much of her time in 2001 developing the impressive Monthly Speakers Roundtable:

January –   The Honorable Patricia Jessamy, Baltimore City State's Attorney

February –   DeWayne Wickham, Board Chairman, Woodholm Foundation

March –   Maurice Tose, President & CEO Telecomminication s System and Tim Smoot, Senior Vice President, Meridian Management Group

April –   James Malone, Men's Health Issues

May –   Barbara Jean Shaneman, LPN, University of Maryland, School of Medicine, Stress & Hypertension

June –   Clarence T. Bishop. Baltimore/Washington Region Region, 2012 Coalition Olympics Ganes

September –   Charles R. Owens, Executive General Manager, Baltimore Afro-American Newspapers

October –   Donna Stanley, Executive Director, Assicated Black Charities

November –   Joint Meeting, Maryland Association of Urban Bankers, Rahn v. Barnes.

December –   2001 BMA Awards Diner, Joy C. Bramble, Publiusher, Baltimore Times Newspapers

Joy C. Bramble, publisher of *The Baltimore Times Newspaper*, was named the thirty-third recipient of the Henry G. Parks, Jr. Business Award. The keynote speaker was The Honorable Alexis M. Herman, Secretary of the U.S. Department of Labor who was the first African American to lead the Labor Department in 1997.

The Baltimore Times Newspaper group began with a simple yet extraordinary goal to counter the negative images often portrayed of African Americans in the media. It highlighted and celebrated the positive contributions made by blacks to their communities, workplaces, churches, and families.

With little more than a dream and the support of her young family, Bramble began printing "positive stories about positive people" in 1986 and watched her company grow from a one-room operation in her kitchen to, at the time, the largest circulated African American publication on the East Coast with more than 200,000 readers in Baltimore, Prince George's County, Annapolis, and the Maryland's Eastern Shore.

Bramble grew up on the Caribbean island of Montserrat where at thirteen-years-old, she hosted one of the island's most popular radio programs. Bramble graduated from Queens University in Ontario, Canada and the University of Calgary in Canada and later taught in Antigua, Connecticut, and Baltimore city schools. Bramble opened two grocery stores in Baltimore and became more convinced than ever that blacks needed to involve themselves in establishing their own institutions through which services, goods, and jobs could be delivered to the community. Thus, *The Baltimore Times* was born.

Bramble sat on numerous boards and commissions, including the University School of Medicine, the Maryland Education Coalition, and Goodwill Industries. Bramble was the founding member of XI Group. It was a web design and technology company. She was a principal partner with Madison Funding, Inc., a Maryland-based mortgage company and a founding member with Madison Real Estate Holdings. Among her proudest accomplishments is founding Times Community Services, Inc., the philanthropic arm of the *Baltimore Times Newspaper*. Bramble was included among Who's Who Business Persons and received countless awards for her contributions to the community (*Archives of The Baltimore Marketing Association, Inc., Program Booklet, Thirty-Third Annual Business Awards Dinner, December 6th, 2001*).

Muldrow also announced that Arthur E. Peterson was awarded the Harold D. Young Esquire Leadership Award in 2001. Petersen had been a member of BMA for eighteen years and served as Vice President of Member Development, Vice President of Program Development, and Chair of BMA Awards Dinner that honored William C. March, founder of March Funeral Homes.

Petersen was also a founder and Charter member of the Maryland Chapter of the National Transportation Officials. For more than twenty-five years, he provided executive

management advisory services to government agencies and businesses that have enabled minority-owned businesses in emerging growth industry sectors, to build their capacity and become more effective competitors as they built their revenues and enhanced their profitability. Petersen acquired a Bachelor's Degree in Urban Studies from Morgan State University and an MBA degree from Atlanta University with a specialty in transportation.

Muldrow culminated his presidency by naming of Dale V. Griffin, the recipient of the Harold Young Esq., Leadership Award. Griffin was the Manager of Visitor Services for the Walters Art Museum in Baltimore city where she trained and supervised front-line personnel and box office staff.

(Archives of The Baltimore Marketing Association, Inc.).

On June 19th, 2003, April Ryan, White House Correspondent with a permanent assignment to the White House Press Corp, spoke at BMA's monthly meeting. Her comments reflected on a time when she attended a meeting with President William ("Bill') Clinton. The occasion was a soul food dinner prepared by Ryan's aunt Pearl in the summer of 1999. It was organized by black correspondents and was attended by President Clinton. The menu was typical of more festive events and certainly cooler temperatures. It included "chitterlings," fried garlic chicken, black-eyed peas, collard greens, cornbread, barbecue ribs, and peach cobbler. Clinton was casual in his conversation, attitude, and attire in the off-record event. However, he did make a formal statement when he responded to the question of why he never apologized for slavery. He said, *"Some of the problem in the black community is that African Americans do not come together on issues."*

The room was filled with black reporters and two White House staffers who sat at a long wooden dinner table. Ryan recalled how she interrupted the President and asked, "Did you all hear that? Because many black people consider him the first black President," he got away with that statement. Ryan commented that he was one of the few white men who were unofficially granted license to make such a comment.

On August 18th, 2003, Margaret Hayes, VP - Membership Development and Michael Easterly, Executive VP, appeared on the "Tina Baldwin Show" to promote The Baltimore Marketing Association, Inc.

September 18th, 2003, BMA had the honor of hosting Penelope J. Taylor, Vice Chairwoman, MBNA America Bank, based in Wilmington, Delaware. Taylor joined MBNA in 1986. Taylor is a graduate of the College of Notre Dame of Maryland, where she received both her Undergraduate and Master's degrees. She is a lifetime member of the NAACP, Maryland Association of Urban Bankers, and member of the Urban Financial Services Coalition.

Taylor spoke at Coppin State University to college students majoring in business, finance, and marketing and a crowd of professionals. Her topic: Setting and resetting your career compass. All sailors know the condition of their vessel at all times.

Our lecturer in October 2003 spoke of his journey from a small town in West Virginia to Corporate Vice President of Rite Aid, one of the largest drug store chains in the nation to launching his own company. His topic was "Niche Markets, Leverage and the Multiplier."

Dr. Dalton is President and CEO of Health Resources, Inc., a pharmacy benefit management company, listed as No. 22 among Black Enterprise Magazine top one hundred businesses.

Dr. Dalton is also President and CEO of UNIVEC Conglomerate, a public-traded company, which manufactures and distributes specialty pharmaceuticals to hospitals, physicians, pharmacies, and clinics nationwide. Physician and Pharmaceutical Services Inc, (PPSI) is the pharmacy sample services division of UNIVEC that provides prescription "Starter-Script" samples for physicians to give to their patients. Dr. Dalton also is the Chairman of the Executive Board of the National Minority Health Association.

Finally, he related how important it is to spend quality time with the family. He measured much of his successes to the support of his family.

In December 2003, Arnold Williams, CPA and Managing Director of Abrams, Foster, Nole, & Williams, PA, was awarded the thirty-fourth Henry G. Parks Jr. Business Award. Williams held an Associate of Arts Degree in Accounting from the Community College of Baltimore and a Bachelor of Science Degree from the University of Baltimore.

For many years, he provided extensive services to local and regional businesses in Baltimore, Washington, D.C., Virginia, and Pennsylvania. He was well-known as a professional whose advisory services were distinguished by a personal touch and sensitivity to client's concerns and needs. Williams served as Chair of the Baltimore Development Corporation (BDC), a non-profit organization which is the economic development agency of Baltimore City. This organization had responsibility for retaining, expanding, and attracting businesses through the facilitation of strategic Baltimore real estate development and construction projects and business support programs. BDC acted as a liaison among city agencies, business owners, and developers to direct private and business growth and development. At the time of his award, Williams served on numerous corporate boards that included being Chair of Bon Secours Baltimore Health System and was appointed by the Governor to the Maryland State Board of Public Accountancy (*Archives of The Baltimore Marketing Association, Inc., Program Booklet, Thirty-Fourth Annual Business Awards Dinner, December 4th, 2003*).

BMA membership had become diversified to include minority business owners, representatives of major corporations, private citizens, and government officials.

As BMA's efforts to enhance its brand as a strong supporter of education through Muldrow's leadership, BMA Adopt-A-School program, adopted Margaret Brent Elementary School (School #53) where Brenda K. Abrams was principal.

The school, located in an urban community named for Margaret Brent, dated back to pre-revolutionary days. The school was named for Margaret Brent, a practicing attorney in colonial Maryland. The original section of the school, on the northeast corner of St. Paul and Twenty-Sixth Streets, was constructed in 1897 and housed kindergarten through eighth-grade students.

In 1919, it was an "all-girls" school and was departmentalize in upper grades.

Brenda K. Abrams, Principal
Margaret Brent Elementary School

That school reflected varied racial, ethnic, and social/economic groups in the communities of Harwood, Remington, and Charles Village. The initial effort was to provide technical support for the school's computer lab. BMA spearheaded a technical assessment of all the technological systems of the school and in partnership with other businesses, was able to host a Virtual Career Day Program at the school for the students (*Archives of The Baltimore Marketing Association, Inc.*).

———————

In December 2004, Diane L. Bell-McKoy was named the recipient of the Henry G. Parks Jr. Business Award. Bell-McKoy was President and CEO of Empower Baltimore Management Corporation (EBMC), the nonprofit organization that managed the Empower Zone in Baltimore city. She won numerous awards and national acclaim when she received a National Best Practice Award by the U.S. Department of Housing and Urban Development. Bell-McKoy was also honored by the Maryland/Washington Minority Contractors and her most distinguished honor was her nomination by the Ford Foundation's "Leadership for a Changing Award."

During her tenure as the President and CEO of EBMC, she was praised for having created 6,603 new jobs, which contributed to more than $1.2 billion in economic activity to the city of Baltimore's economy. Those 6,603 jobs were combined with 4,012 jobs that were created through the "spin-off" or "multiplier effects" for a total employment impact of 10,615 city jobs that were supported by the Baltimore Empowerment Zone job creation programs. There was an estimated $455 million in salaries and wages that were associated with those jobs. The economic activity, supported by the Empowerment Zone, generated an estimated $21 million in State sales and income taxes, and $21.3 million in city income and property taxes.

From 1994 to 2004, EBMC was successful in leveraging its federal designation of being an Empowerment Zone by creating 5,777 new jobs and retaining an additional 826 jobs for Baltimore city residents. The total number of jobs that were directly linked to the programs and activities of the EZ were most likely undercounted.

Using the total federal funds that were spent for job creation, EBMC spent an average of $3,917 per job that were created or retained from 1994 to 2004. EBMC spent an average of $4,103 of funding from all sources on job creation per job that was created or retained from 1994 to 2004. The Small Business Administration used a benchmark of $35,000 spent per job creation. Using that benchmark, EBMC was very effective in leveraging its job creation efforts in Baltimore city (*Archives of The Baltimore Marketing Association, Inc, Program Booklet, Thirty-Fifth Annual Business Awards Dinner, December 2nd, 2004.*).

In 2004, Frank Coakley was named recipient of the Harold D. Young, Esquire Leadership award. Coakley received that award because of the important work he undertook at the Fannie Mae Baltimore Partnership Office, managing over 1.2 billion over a five-year period. Coakley served BMA for over twenty-two years as Vice President of Membership, Treasurer, and Board of Directors. Prior to joining Fannie Mae, Coakley had an illustrious career as the Assistant Secretary and Director of the Community Development Administration. Coakley used his finance and business acumen gained over many years of service to improve the financial standing of BMA (*Archives of The Baltimore Marketing Association, Inc.*).

Nicholas T. Abrams, Financial Advisor of the Nationwide Financial Network, specialized in wealth management for individuals and corporations and became the BMA President in 2005.

Abrams efficiently managed BMA through strict delegation of duties with a "no nonsense" management style of leadership. He immediately put his membership and board to work and had an impressive first year in the presidency. Abrams announced during his administration that BMA had awarded over $140,000 in scholarships to students who were attending HBCU's in Maryland (*Archives of The Baltimore Marketing Association, Inc.*).

He appointed an Award's Committee charged with vetting the thirty-sixth Henry G. Parks Jr. Business Award nominees. When Abrams learned of the results among the nominees, he immediately contacted Dr. Tyrone D. Taborn, Chair and CEO of Career Communications Group, Inc.

Tyrone Taborn enjoyed a multi-faceted career as a businessman and advocate for broadening diversity in America's technical and scientific workforce and to educate minority youth. One supporter wrote, *"[Y]our selection is indicative of your persistent dedication to our youth, unrelenting pursuit of excellence and unsurpassed professionalism."*

Tabor had been an op-ed page writer for the Baltimore Sun Papers and had been a panelist on the television program, "Square Off," at WJZ-TV, the CBS affiliate in Baltimore. Taborn was the founder of Family Tech Week program, which was sponsored by the IBM Corporation. Taborn was also selected to receive the Hispanic Engineer of the Year Chairman Award and was one of nine Internet and technology leaders honored by Sprint and MOBE IT, which recognized Minority leaders and geniuses in technology (*Archives of The Baltimore Marketing Association, Inc, Program Booklet, Thirty-Sixth Annual Business Awards Dinner, December 2nd, 2005*).

At the 2005 Awards Dinner, Margaret A. Hayes was named recipient of the Harold D. Young, Esquire Leadership Award.

Hayes joined BMA in 2002 and served on the technology committee, the Awards Dinner Committee, the Vice President of Membership, and Executive Vice President's committees.

In 1977, Hayes joined the University of Maryland School of Pharmacy and served as Director of Student Educational Services and Faculty Academic Advisor. She co-taught the Student Leadership and Advisory course. During the spring of 2004, she encouraged a group of UMB Pharmacy students, the Student Section of Maryland Public Health Association, to address healthcare disparities.

Hayes was Executive Director of a Bridge to Academic Excellence (ABAE), a middle/high school tutoring program. This program was designed for students who had difficulty in math and the sciences. Under her leadership, she formed partnerships with several organizations, including the Girl Scouts and the Erickson Foundation's Harbor Academic Program.

She was recognized as one of Maryland's Top 100 Women in 2005 and was also recognized for her outstanding community service by the U.S. Air Force, Lambda Kappa Sigma International Professional Pharmacy Fraternity at the University of Maryland's Baltimore and Diversity Recognition Award for ABAE (*Archives of The Baltimore Marketing Association, Inc.*).

———————

In December 2006, Nicholas T. Abrams and his team looked for business organizations with deep roots in the African American business community that would meet the stringent requirements of past Henry G. Parks Jr. honorees. BMA selected March Funeral Homes, owners of one of the largest African American-owned funeral service companies in the United States. The March family started their business in 1957 in a single row house on East North Avenue in Baltimore. The business grew steadily grew until 1978 when the firm moved to a newly constructed funeral home that occupied an entire city block. In 1985, the March family built a second facility in West Baltimore.

It was founded by the late William C. March and his business partner and wife of fifty-nine years, the late Julia Roberta March. March Funeral Homes received numerous awards and recognition as a leader in the industry not only for its innovation but for a commitment to providing dignified funeral services for everyone, regardless of their financial situation.

In 1992, the family, under the leadership of their children, acquired full ownership of King Memorial Park in Baltimore County and expanded the cemetery to 155 acres, making the cemetery the largest black-owned cemetery in the country.

Thanks to their parents' business savvy and ensuing successes, all of the March children were able to attend and complete a college education – a long-wished-for goal that fueled William's and Julia's determination and drive.

Annette and Cynthia March became registered nurses while Erich opted for a degree in psychology at the Johns Hopkins. Victor graduated from Loyola University with a degree in accounting and became a CPA. He later attended Harvard Business School's Presidential Management Program. With many civic affiliations, including the Board of Directors of Cerebral Palsy of Central Maryland and the united Negro College Fund, Julia Roberta March instilled in her children the importance of community involvement and giving back.

The March family established the Thelma March Scholarship Foundation in honor of Mr. March's sister to provide scholarships for college-bound students from Dunbar and Douglass High Schools. According to Victor, he and his siblings all envisioned different career paths and enjoyed their ability to "fly solo" for a while. However, each knew deep down that they would eventually make their way back to the family business. As children growing up in the funeral business, living above the parlor did not seem abnormal. It was well engrained in them at an early age that the business was family and the family was business. Those sentiments could not be separated.

Cynthia March Malloy, a graduate from the University of Maryland in College Park, was a registered nurse and became a licensed mortician in Maryland in 1977. Malloy was the Vice-President of Marcorp, LTD and served on the board of directors. She lived in Richmond, which presented the March children an opportunity to expand the business in another state. As Vice-President and General Manager of the March Funeral Home, the Laburnum Chapel continued to grow and carry the reputation of the March Family.

Erich W. March, Vice President for Funeral Services for Marcorp LTD and President of King Memorial Park, also served on the Board of Directors. He was the past president of the Maryland State Board of Funeral Directors and attended Mortuary School and became licensed in Maryland. Erich and his father, William, were among other founders of Harbor Bank of Maryland.

Victor C. March Sr. was the CEO and Senior Vice President of Marcorp LTD. He also served on the Board of Directors. As a CPA working for Coopers & Lybrand, before leaving to work for the family business in 1979, he became the company's first comptroller. After that role, he became the Vice President of March Funeral Home West, Inc.

Annette March-Grier, Vice President of Public Relations and Marketing and Secretary of King Memorial Park, also served on the board of directors.

She became a licensed mortician in 1985. Annette is a Facilitator and Director of Programs for March Funeral Homes.

(*Archives of The Baltimore Marketing Association, Inc, Program Booklet, Thirty-Seventh Annual Business Awards Dinner, December 7th, 2006*).

Joshua L. Pruden was named recipient of the Harold D. Young, Esquire Leadership Award in 2006. Pruden served the Baltimore City Public Schools since 1984, first as a music teacher and later as a counselor, yet for the most part his objectives had remained the same. He fostered an emotionally-healthy school learning environment while helping children to gain an understanding of self, a positive attitude, confidence, and all-important decision-making skills, remained high on Pruden's list of career goals.

With a Bachelor's degree in Music Education from New England Conservatory of Music in Boston, a Master's degree in Adult and Continuing Education from Coppin State University, and a Master's degree in School Counseling from the Johns Hopkins University, it was easy to see how Pruden had successfully intertwined his passion for music and education with his interest in counseling students to shape their future careers.

Pruden served as Executive Secretary of the Baltimore Marketing Association and was an integral member of several committees that produced BMA's Annual Business Awards Dinners.

The Ex Officio President

Every organization has one who serves in Ex Officio capacities. This person, usually working behind the scenes, provides unofficial imperceptible leadership.

Kenneth R. Taylor, Jr. graduated from Morgan with a Bachelor of Science Degree in Business Administration in 1971. In 1977, one year prior to joining BMA, while employed with the Maryland Department of Transportation, Taylor designed and implemented the first public transit bus route directly to Morgan State University. Prior to the implementation of the 33 bus route, public transportation was unreliable and caused many students to arrive late for classes. Routing the bus along Coldspring Lane also provided better transit service for students attending Baltimore Polytechnic Institute and Western High Schools.

Taylor joined BMA 1978 and immediately lent his professional skills perfected in logistics and project management. Harnessing his professional skills, Taylor gained access to high-level officials at Baltimore City Hall. As Vice President of Government Affairs, he facilitated several successful BMA initiatives with the city.

When personal computers became widely available in the 1980s, Taylor became BMA's in-house technical computer advisor. His skills helped BMA members to efficiently use computer programs and applications, and Taylor was later appointed Chairman of the BMA's Website.

Taylor also served as BMA's official host and coordinated meetings, accommodation, and transportation for event speakers. When a BMA monthly meeting location was no longer available, Taylor moved the meeting to the St. Paul School for Girls where he served as Vice Chairman on the Board of Directors.

In 2003, Taylor joined BMA's Board and was later elevated to Chairman of the Board. During his tenure he was recognized for implementing better accountability, programmatic and financial protocols. Whether the changes he made were bold or minimal, Taylor's approach was the same: logically framed and thoughtfully evaluated.

Concurrently, while holding numerous BMA offices, Taylor was recognized by the state of Maryland for his operating and capital budget expertise, and ability to facilitate inter-departmental and inter-jurisdictional cooperation. He distinguished himself as the Vice Chairman, Appellate Judicial Nominating Commission, State of Maryland.

Taylor was Montgomery County's Office of Business Relations and Compliance First Manager. During his tenure he drafted and implemented new legislation for both the County's Local Small Business Reserve Program and the Minority, Female and Disable Persons Program. During his leadership, small and minority business contracting exceeded 20% and the number of contracts awarded small and minority business increased 300% for the first time.

Taylor has now become Ex Officio President of the Baltimore Marketing Association Alumni. He convenes periodic informal meetings, open to all BMA members, usually at member's home or informal locations to discuss BMA nostalgia and current events.

Epilogue

From December 2006 through 2008, BMA's monthly membership meetings and community activities slowly but assuredly came to an end. Through the advent of social media, interest in an organization with structured meeting dates, times, and places to meet began to wane significantly.

Gone were the channels of its younger members' professional development through interpersonal and face-to-face interactions. Members' regular visits to primary and secondary public schools, which served as living witnesses of the successes of professionals in marketing, sales, management, and public relations, eventually ceased. The allure of engaging stories of women and minority business owners gave way to the arrival of new and modern discourses – multitasking, tweets, podcasts, Instagram, emails, and texts.

Social media now allows professionals to use many new tools for personal development with fewer personal social interactions. One can now be engaged in conversations with thousands of individuals on any given day and on any given subject though social media contacts. One can accomplish so much more through our smartphones that we never could have imagined when BMA opened its doors for business in 1967. The enormity of the power-shift to social media can only be compared to the growth of powerful microcomputers as noted: *"Your smartphone is millions of times more powerful than all of NASA's computing in 1969 – the year that man first set foot on the moon" (ZME Science Magazine, February 15th, 2019).*

Reflecting on his vision for BMA when he was elected President in 2005, Nicholas Abrams, last president, was hopeful that new, younger members would lay the foundation for the future of BMA. According Abrams, the task proved more formidable than he ever imagined. Abrams stated, *"I soon found out the people in my age group were not interested in sitting through a meeting, listening to speakers. We were in the age of technology, conference calls, webinars, and emails. Many of the younger members of BMA wanted to change our monthly meetings to quarterly meetings. Communication was becoming more virtual and BMA began feeling the effects of it."*

BMA lost long-cherished business and personal relationships to technology. The handshake, smile, and other nonverbal clues added meaning and assurance to business endeavors and personal commitments but have since become less and less a part of our business lexicon.

Aristotle wrote, *"There can be no words without images."* Plato gave his sense of the importance of being able to physically inspect the subject about what we are commiserating when he wrote, *"Of all the senses, trust only the sense of sight."*

When BMA held its meetings on the third Thursday of each month for forty-one years, members' conversations of the evening sounded like this: "I see your point, let me see, we're not seeing eye to eye, and see what I mean?" Smartphones and millennials changed forever the one essential mode of communicating face-to-face encounters of BMA members and its partners.

Out of the five founding members of BMA – Roland Henson, Ackneil M. Muldrow II, Gary Reynolds, John Rich, and Eugene Smith, only Eugene Smith has survived as a retired business owner of EMS Limousine, Inc. He has a fleet of limousines that services the District of Columbia Virginia, and Maryland (DMV).

In a recent interview, Smith said, *"If you needed to make connections with other professionals, BMA's monthly meeting was the place to be. If you were looking for a job or to make an important contact for your business, the breadth of talent, coupled with some members who were uniquely positioned, created for African Americans, a reservoir of technical assistance, mentoring, guidance and access to 'rolodexes' of influence throughout Maryland."*

BMA was the premier organization for young African Americans in business, management, marketing, and human relations. Those earlier employment ventures helped several BMA members to break through the glass ceilings of corporate America. Many BMA members have since launched their own businesses and expanded their careers in financial planning, transportation, mortgage and commercial lending, insurance, investment banking, real estate development, technology, radio broadcasting, academic administration at the college and university levels, and have become elective representatives of local government.

For forty-one years, members of BMA were dedicated to the principles of the organization—to advance their careers, provide college scholarships, and recognize outstanding accomplishments of local businesswomen and businessmen, which served as the backdrop for the creation of the Black Business Hall of Fame. No doubt these milestones were met with rigorous work and unrelenting commitment.

Latest group picture of members of The Baltimore Marketing Association, Inc. (circa 2003).

The planning meetings of the Executive Board were held on the first Thursday of each month in preparation for the general membership meetings on the third Thursday of the month. Every third Thursday of the month meant Vice Presidents of finance, student affairs, activities, public information, membership and planning, and entertainment were observed hurriedly brushing up their required monthly presentations. Absences of vice presidents from the meetings were permitted, but presentations of monthly reports were required even if made by understudies.

Eleven years after BMA closed its doors, several former BMA members, who have since retired, still meet each first Thursday of the month to discuss current events but mostly to reminisce about the historical characters and events of the organization. Borrowing from the millennials, Kenneth R. Taylor Jr., the most technologically-gifted of the retired members, sends an email or texts each month as a reminder several days before each meeting.

There continues to be an indisputable fraternal bond among many members, extending to family relations, church, and social activities. Plato's theory of communication, being physical present in the moment, still looms large among the BMA alumni. The conversations at the meetings on the first of each month could very well occur through social media. Instead former BMA members still prefer to physically see persons with whom they would be commiserating. These members "trust only the sense of sight" and enjoy the face-to-face interaction and the give and take in the presence of each other.

Recalling his tenure as BMA's last president, Abrams chose to embrace the value of the organization to young African American professionals of his generation and generation before him, stating that "its legacy continues in the Baltimore area." (*Archives of The Baltimore Marketing Association, Inc.*).

APPENDIX I

A Course of Action for the Corporate Minority Relations Program

by
Ackneil M. Muldrow, II

Corporate managers have gained considerable expertise, over the years, in dealing with their various publics. Whether their attention is directed to employees, plant com-

Muldrow

munities, customers or stockholders, they have learned successful guidelines which help formulate corporate policy. If the public were an unchanging and monolithic entity, corporate relations could possibly be handled by rote. But fortunately, publics regroup and public opinion changes more rapidly and is more influential than ever before. And this is the continuing challenge that keeps corporate management alert to new needs and new opportunities.

Just such a challenge confronts management in formulating and effectively administrating a corporate minority relations program. A large part of the program is, of course, devoted to equal opportunity employment—and this, in itself, goes far beyond the written words of Title VII of the 1964 Civil Rights Bill. It includes a corporate policy of non-discrimination . . . it involves a commitment to these objectives by those who have hiring and other personnel responsibilities . . . and it requires the cooperation of co-workers as well as supervisory staff members. This part of the program must begin at the top. To be effective, it must filter throughout the organization.

An ineffective program is hardly better than no program at all. Members of minority groups have been seeing the phrase "an equal opportunity employer" in help wanted ads for five years. Yet, to many of these

people, the phrase carries a hollow, meaningless ring. These are the people who have applied for "equal opportunity employment" only to be discouraged or summarily rejected by a receptionist. These are the people who have been hired, then given a

The author of this article, Ackneil M. Muldrow, II, joined Commercial Credit Corp. in 1966 following several years service in retail management, and in counseling in the Baltimore, Md. public schools. His first assignment with the sales finance and personal loan firm, as Personnel Administrator, required extensive traveling throughout the country to visit Commercial Credit offices. During this time, he was instrumental in clarifying and implementing the company's Equal Employment policies. In 1968, he was promoted to Coordinator of Equal-Employment Opportunity. Muldrow is a graduate of North Carolina A&T State University in Greensboro, N.C. and is a member of the Baltimore Jaycees, Baltimore Marketing Association, NAACP, and Toastmaster's International.

prominent location in a department where the "work" taxes their ability to look busy. These are the people who become part of a work force, but never enjoy the fraternity with others that makes working enjoyable.

Total Involvement

This is why equal opportunity employment requires total involvement. And total involvement requires a comprehensive communication program, and periodic re-evaluation, to make sure that the program is really working—not just creating a pleasant veneer.

A minority relations program includes other areas of activity and assistance. Programs sponsored by the National Alliance for Business and Job Opportunities, for example, present challenges for training hard-core persons. In many cases, this can be an up-hill task; but on the other side of the coin, many companies have been gratified by the success of their help in readying more and more people for gainful employment.

Specially Written Literature For Inner City Students

Education is important, too, and meaningful literature written especially for inner city primary and secondary school students can be most helpful in introducing them to the world of money, banking and finance —and teaching them some of the principles of personal money management. Educators are particularly receptive to properly prepared materials which help them make this subject make sense. And, as a collateral service, guided tours of company facilities dramatize the importance of business to class members.

To be really successful, a minority relations program should involve leaders in the minority community itself—organizations such as the American Indian's Council, NAACP, Operation Breadbasket, Opportunities Industrialization Center (OIC), Puerto Rico Labor Department and the Urban League are staffed with knowledgeable persons who can provide worthwhile advice and serve as liaison with the minority community. And this is vitally important if the program is going to be meaningful.

We at Commercial Credit feel that our minority relations program wouldn't have been as successful as it is without the assistance of the dedicated people who direct activities for

INDUSTRIAL BANKER *Reprinted by permission.*

minority organizations. What we are trying to do is bridge the gap between blacks and whites, not only in the field of finance, but in the community as a whole. Our program not only applies to our home office, but is a vital part of Commercial Credit's field operations as well. And it includes a total awareness and involvement by all of our employees.

The involvement extends to our affiliated companies, too. Well managed and financially sound Negro banks, for example, are considered for account relationships and insurance companies in the Commercial Credit group are participating in building low income housing in ghetto areas.

It's true that inner-city ghettos simply have not had the essential characteristics for wide-spread marketing of financial services. But we've learned that the minority community has its plus factors, too: pleasant residential areas; well managed banks, insurance companies and other businesses; and concerned citizens who send their children to Negro colleges and universities with high academic standards as well as other institutions of higher learning.

Within this community there is an undeveloped resource of human talent, energy and ambition. There is a capacity for leadership and an untested opportunity for economic growth.

Is It Worthwhile?

Is a minority relations program worthwhile? Let's consider some of the benefits. First of all, there's the altruistic reasoning which includes the responsibilities of successful businesses in being good corporate citizens by improving the economic status of deprived human beings. Then there's the more businesslike point of view in utilizing this untapped source of employable people. And, of course, there's the long range view which recognizes the future business relationships which will prove to be mutually profitable as this community becomes stronger and more financially sound.

At Commercial Credit, we don't feel that our minority relations program has been an exercise of social welfare. We look on it as an investment in our future. And our program has begun to pay dividends already.

APPENDIX II

Last Directors and Officers of The Baltimore Marketing Association, Inc.

Board of Directors
Ackneil M. Muldrow, II, Chairman
Nicolas T. Abrams
Frank B. Coakley
Joshua L. Pruden
Charles T. Robinson, Sr.
Kenneth R. Taylor, Jr.
Craig A. Thompson, Esquire
Teaira Brooks-Turner

Officers
Nicolas T. Abrams, President & CEO
Margaret A. Hayes, M.S. Executive Vice President
Joshua L. Pruden, Executive Secretary
Frank B. Coakley, Treasurer
Craig A. Thompson, Esquire, General Counsel

Standing Committees (Vice Presidents)

Gloria griffin -Education Committee
Cynthia T. DeJesus – Entertainment Committee
Monique K. Booker – Finance Committee
Tracine Andres – Membership Development Committee
Rodney E. Taylor – Program Development Committee
Penny McCrimmon – Public Affairs Committee
Ad-hoc Committees

Kenneth R. Taylor, Jr. – Chairman Website
Harold D. Young, Esquire – Chairman, Black Business Hall of Fame

The Black Business Hall of Fame

A committee chaired by Harold D. Young worked for several years to establish the Black Business Hall of Fame in 1982. It was designed to pay tribute to Maryland African American business owners who made major contributions in business and industry. Young said during one of its organizational meetings that, *"Black business owners had made major contributions in business and industry in this nation and state…we must never forget to remember the great talents displayed by blacks against adverse circumstances…and enshrining such businesspersons in BMA's Hall of Fame is a noble thing to do."*

The inductees would be enshrined after the credentials of the nominees had been validated and the structure of the Black Business Hall of Fame was formally established. Biennially, African American business owners who were enshrined in the Hall of Fame would have demonstrated significant contributions as business owners and for their contributions to their communities. These men and women of extraordinary courage and faith would have persevered against challenging and daunting circumstances of their efforts.

Hall of Fame inductees served as beacons of hope for many business aspirants. The Baltimore Marketing Association celebrated African American pioneers in business and industry to preserves their place in history because of its strong belief in the values of rediscovering our past for posterity.

Muldrow proudly remarked during the first Hall of Fame Induction Ceremony that *"By studying the lives of these unique business personalities, you will better understand the depth of the pride that spirited these individuals to overcome circumstances and rise victoriously in their fight to uplift blacks around the state."*

The Baltimore Marketing Association paid tribute to black business men and business women whose works represented: (1) Significant periods of history (2) pioneering business (3) outstanding human attributes, or (4) were currently operating a business. Further, each inductee must not only have made outstanding business accomplishments but should have also shown high standards of responsibility to their respective communities. Biennially, BMA enshrined black business persons by telling their stories of a proud people because it understood and strongly believed in the vlaue of rediscovering its past to make sure that its youth knew of the great black pioneers in business who had laid pathways for them to follow.

The Baltimore Marketing Association, Inc.

Salutes

The Black Business Hall of Fame Inductees

Pauline B. Brooks (1915 – 1996)

Robert W. Coleman (1877 – 1946)

Josiah Diggs (1864 – 1938)

John H. Murphy, Sr. (1840 – 1922)

Isaac Myers (1835 – 1891)

Henry G. Parks, Jr. (1916 – 1989)

Charles Shipley (1879 – 1943)

Nelson Wells (1786 – 1843)

T. Wallis Lansey (1883 – 1948),

Roger Sanders (Died March 31, 1998)

Walter T. Dixon (1893 – 1980)

Camilla White Sherrard

Thomas H. Kerr (1888 – 1985)

"Captain" George W. Brown (Died November 27, 1935)

William L. Adams (January 14, 1914 – June 27, 2011)

Harry A. Carpenter (September 6, 1885 – Januayr 24, 2003)

Anthony Thomas (1857 – 1931)

Dr. Joseph H. Thomas (1885 – 1963)

Charles Thurgood Burns (1914 – 1991)

Raymond V. Haysbert, Sr. (1902 – 2010)

Parren J. Mitchell (April 29, 1922 – May 28, 2007)

Allen Quille (August 17, 1919 – January 1, 2002)

Kenneth O. Wilson (November 5, 1918 – June 17, 2004)

Deaver Young Smith, Sr. (August 24, 1890 – January 1975)

Carroll Henry Hynson (Died December 19, 1994)

Benjamin L. King (Died March 15, 2005)

Roosevelt Nixon (January 1926 – November 22, 1972)

Reginald F. Lewis (December 7, 1942 – January 19, 1993)

Eddie C. Brown

1982

Pauline B. Brooks (1915-1996) had a penchant for sales. As a youngster, she sold Christmas cards, even offering sale prices for customers who wanted special gold printing, and when she became older, she sold stockings and undergarments. Her next venture was selling cosmetics for a company that was owned and operated by two black women in the late 1940s.

Brooks was born in Staunton, Virginia. She moved to Baltimore with her parents when she was five and later graduated from Douglass High School during the depression in 1933. Her dream of becoming a teacher was cut short when she began working as a "house manager" for a divorced mother who was living alone. She continued taking courses in sewing and corseting. Later she worked in clothing stores and attended Cortez Peters Business School at night.

Brooks' sense of style drew the attention of the store owners where she worked and was later promoted as a buyer. When Brooks went to New York, many of the manufactures consulted with her on a particular dress or designer line. She subsequently developed a personal line of clothing following of her own. At the prompting of friends and her customers, she considered opening a clothing store of her own.

At a time when department stores did not always allow blacks to try on clothes before purchase and had to shop in black communities that generally sold garments at considerably lesser qualities, Brooks, with personal funds and a $500 loan from the Equitable Bank, opened a small dress shop on the upper level of Mondawmin Mall in Baltimore to offer fashionable clothing for black women. Her shop was the place for black women to find something chic and unique that no one else would be wearing. She was a trendsetter for a lot of boutiques that catered to blacks. Later on she relocated her store to the elegant Belvedere Hotel on Chase Street.

Brooks' role as a mother and businesswoman began simultaneously with the diligent help of her husband where she managed a new business and a new baby. Unfortunately, three years later, her husband died. She had every reason to give up, yet she bore her trials and maintained her faith believing that God would help her through it all.

Easy-going by nature, Brooks was humble and unassuming. She believed in hard work and in providing top-quality products. She maintained that the challenge of her day for black people was to learn loyalty to one another. She believed that blacks can do anything they wanted to do if they had respect for each other and a sense of obligation. Practicing what she preached, Brooks acted on her faith in God.

Pauline Brooks was a member of the *Clever Kiquejays*, a group dedicated to preserving the memory of Robert W. Coleman who was a Baltimore businessman noted for his work with handicapped persons. She was a member of Douglass Community Church, the YMC, and a member of the Council for Equal Business Opportunities (CEBO).

Robert W. Coleman (1877-1946) was a businessman who produced the *Colored Directory* in Baltimore, Maryland.

In the early 1900s, black people went to the nearest drug store, paid fifty cents, and took home the directory. It was the Black Pages of that time and listed all black-owned and operated businesses in Baltimore. For twenty-seven years, this was the main business venture of Coleman who owned and operated his business while he was blind.

Coleman was born in Washington, D.C. in November 1877 and moved to Baltimore at age nineteen. He later took a job as a valet with a very wealthy man on Charles Street near the Belvedere Hotel. His employer, Mr. Wilde, was related to Wallace Warfield Simpson, the future Duchess of Windsor. Unfortunately, Coleman had to give up this job when he began to lose his sight.

He attended the Maryland Workshop for the Blind where he developed hobbies of piano-tuning and hammock-making, which he developed into a business. It was at that workshop where he witnessed discrimination toward the colored blind and endeavored to do something about it.

In 1913, when little attention was given to the needs of the handicapped, he, with the help of some friends, established The Maryland Association for the Colored Blind. The group's objectives were to improve the religious, moral, social, educational, industrial, economical, and physical conditions for the colored blind. This association is still active today, developing and implementing activities that aid many individuals, particularly children. Every year on George Washington's birthday, Coleman honored the deaf, blind, and crippled children at Sharp Street Methodist Church. This was an inspiring gathering. He also started the SAVE A SIGHT CAMPAIGNS to provide glasses for needy children.

Coleman touched many people with his boundless energy. When an idea inspired him, it could not escape him until he had seen it through. He has been described as a man with contagious enthusiasm. He had a gentle nature that was moved by distresses and hardships of others. It was his love for mankind and faith in his race that were his motivating forces. He was known for his celestial smile and inner peace born of his grounded faith in God.

Coleman's wife, Mary Mason Coleman, whom he always referred to as "his right arm," and his daughters were an integral part of the *Directory* business. They remembered him as a warm and giving man dedicated to the growth and development of his people. An elementary school located in the 2300 block of Windsor Avenue was named after Coleman.

Josiah Diggs (1864-1938). Following the end of World War I, Diggs made a pioneering breakthrough by becoming the first black man to own and operate a Moving Picture Parlor. The fact that such a business would have come to mind of a black man in those days when "service" oriented businesses were the norm was testimony to a pattern of innovated thinking and courage found in Josiah Diggs' life.

Diggs opened his Dunbar Theatre, which was named after Paul Lawrence Dunbar, in East Baltimore. The theatre was located along the Washington Street "black belt," which grew in population during wartime when many blacks were lured to Baltimore by war-time production opportunities. The theatre seated 350 people. Six years after its opening, Diggs tore down the building and built a new theatre at 619-623 Central Avenue. He then hired a seven-piece orchestra, and between 200 and 750 people paid five cents every day to see two performances.

Early in life, Diggs began delivering coal, wood, and ice from the business in which he operated from the back of his 2040 Druid Hill Avenue residence at one time with his grandson, Walter Carr Sr. As editor of the Nite Life tabloid, Carr was prominent in the business world, known for his sense of honesty and personal integrity. He was loved by those who knew him as a modest and courageous personality with kind, gentle, courtly, and dignified manners.

Diggs was a member and trustee of Bethel A.M.E. Church, a grand keeper of the records and seal of the Knights of Pythias-Masonic Order for twenty-nine years, treasurer of Provident Hospital, YMCA board member, treasurer of the board of directors at the Association for the Handicapped, advisory board member for the Camp for the Underprivileged Children and the Vocational School. Diggs was an activist as he routinely picketed businesses that refused to employ blacks. He was best known for his philanthropic endeavors, and every Christmas, he provided food baskets for 100 needy families in the city and personally visited those families. During the winter, mothers packed dinners and took their children to the theatre after school in the evenings. The theatre was heated, but many of their homes were not. Diggs was a devout Christian, and he felt giving was his responsibility since he was obviously blessed.

Diggs' family was important to him, and dinner in his home was a formal affair. It did not imply that he was a stiff-neck or had a stern, turn-of-the-century personality that might have come to mind. He was quite the opposite. His grandson remembered him as a smiling, dapper, light on his feet fellow who might dance into the kitchen while juggling dishes. His foresight was extraordinary to think that in 1935, he spoke of the revolutionary effects of the experimental movie box called a television, which would be the movies' major competitor.

John H. Murphy Sr. (1840-1922) was a former slave set free by the Maryland Emancipation Act of 1863. He purchased at auction the name and printing equipment of a small one page weekly going out of business. That publication was known as the *Afro-American Newspaper*. At the time of his new enterprise, only 5.7 percent of the 216,00 black Baltimoreans were considered literate. In 1829, only half of the 68,409 black school-aged children were enrolled in school.

When president Lincoln issued a call for colored troops in the Civil War, Murphy (then twenty-four) enlisted in Company G of the 30th Regiment Infantry U.S. Colored Troops, Maryland Volunteers, and rose to the rank of First Sergeant. After the war, Murphy returned to Baltimore and married Martha Howard of Montgomery County, Maryland.

Murphy's first venture in the newspaper business was the Sunday School Helper, which he set up and printed himself to create interest in Sunday School work. During that time, Murphy was District Sunday School Superintendent of the Hagerstown District of the A.M.E. Church. Murphy was a member of fraternal organizations but worked hardest for the Shriners of which he became Imperial Potentate. He was a member of the board of managers of Provident Hospital and a president of the Negro Press Association and member of the National Business League in the early 1990s and was also President of the Negro Publishers Association. Murphy remained the publisher of *The Afro* for thirty years until his death in 1922. He left his children what was then the largest black newspaper plant in the country operated and manned by 138 employees with a circulation of 14,000.

He often remarked to his sons, whom he brought into the business, "I have faith in myself, in the ability of my people to succeed in this civilization, and in the ultimate justice, which will secure them full citizenship in the nation. I measure a newspaper not in buildings, equipment and employees, those trimmings. A newspaper succeeds because its management believes in itself, in God, and in the present generation. It must always ask itself whether it has kept faith with the common people, whether it has no other goal, except to see that their liberties are preserved and their future assured, whether it is fighting to get rid of slums, to provide jobs for everybody."

When Isaac Myers (1835-1891) was born, Nelson Wells was at the height of his business activities of acquiring real estate and making other personal investments. The colored people of Baltimore managed to have ten churches, ninety institutions for mutual relief, and a number of schools, even though the environment was often oppressive.

Myers received a common school education. At the age of sixteen, he was apprentice to James Jackson, a prominent colored man of his day, who taught him the trade of ship caulking. At the age of twenty, he was superintending the caulking of some of the largest clipper ships being built.

In 1865, Baltimore saw the great strike against colored mechanics and longshoreman. More than 1,000 men were driven from employment. Facing this obstacle, Myers met the challenge by applying a simple premise, "Let's start our own shipyard and marine railway." Myers proposed the idea to a number of merchants who promised their support. He called meetings in all the colored churches of Baltimore, organized a company, and within months, raised $10,000 cash by selling $5 shares exclusively to colored people. Later the organizers bought Muller's yard and railway for $40,000 and 300 colored caulkers and carpenters found immediate employment. The Chesapeake Marine and Railway Dry Dock Company was formed in 1866. It was located near the entrance of the Jones Falls at Fells Point where it operated for eighteen years, securing many government contracts.

In 1870, Myers received a commission as special agent to supervise the mail service in the Southern states. His travels in the South made him vulnerable to Ku Klux Klan attacks, many times narrowly escaping their assaults. After retiring from the railyard in 1882, he was the was editor and proprietor of the "Colored Citizens," a weekly campaign newspaper. In 1888, Myers organized the Maryland Colored State Industrial Fair Associates, the Colored Business Men's Association of Baltimore, and the first colored building and loan association. The Journal of Negro History, Vol. LIX, No.1, January 1974.

Other activities that Myers championed included having authored a *Masonic Digest* and wrote a drama in three acts named "The Missioner." Myers was also Trustee and Secretary of the Board of Bethel A.M.E. Church.

Henry G. Parks Jr. (1916-1989) was a positive personality who was thought of as a marketing genius, known for saying, "You don't get anything by being negative. As a salesperson, you have to count the sales you make, not the ones you lose." This positive personality is reflected in his life. He built a small sausage company into a multi-million-dollar business.

The Parks products were sold in over 12,000 stores from Massachusetts to Virginia. Although commonly referred to as the Parks Sausage Company, its corporate identity was *H.G. Parks, Inc.*

Parks was born in Atlanta Georgia and moved with his parents to Dayton, Ohio when he was six-months-old. There he grew up under a strong family and the religious influence of his grandmother. After graduating from Roosevelt High School in Dayton, he attended Ohio State University. His roommate during college was Jesse Owens, the great Olympic track star. After graduating from Ohio State with a degree in marketing, he learned that there were no jobs in marketing for blacks.

Dr. Mary McLeod Bethune, a deep influence in Parks' life, assisted him to obtain a job managing a War Production and Training Center during World War II. Meanwhile, he wrote a marketing proposal for the Pabst Brewing Company, whose popular brand was Pabst Blue Ribbon Beer. The proposal focused on marketing specifically to the black consumer market. He ultimately went to work for Pabst and became its top sales representative but was never given the opportunity to be the sales manager. Later he decided he would go into the advertising and booking agency business with an associate.

One of the acts he booked was Marva Louis, the wife of the boxing great, Joe Louis. Through Joe Louis, he met a group of businessmen in Baltimore who were impressed with his energy and agreed to go into business with him. One of those persons was William L. Adams, who invested in a sausage company in Ohio. Parks sold their interest and returned to Baltimore when the original owner of the business didn't want to expand. While working for that company, he had set up a small processing plant in Baltimore and acquired a space in the rear of 2509 Pennsylvania Avenue, established a business, and thus began the Parks Sausage Company.

Years later Parks needed to expand to compete with other of meat processing companies. However, time after time, his requests for loans were rejected with bank officers not telling him exactly why. Through his relations among local businesses, Parks was finally able to secure two loans from the Maryland National Bank and the Monumental Life Insurance Company that resulted in a well-designed modern structure in the Camden Industrial Park in south Baltimore on West Hamburg Street. The company moved into its new plant and offices in 1964.

Parks appeared on the cover of Business Week in January in 1968. Soon thereafter he joined the board of directors of First Pennsylvania Corporation, Black Enterprise Magazine, Board of Advisors, Magnavox, W. R. Grace and Company, and Warner Lambert. Parks was also a member of Macrodyne Industries, the Signal Corporation and the Urban National Corporation, an investment capital concern. One year later, in 1969, Parks took Parks Sausage public, and it became the first African American firm listed on the New York Stock Exchange.

In 1977, Parks sold his sausage manufacturer to the Norin Corporation of Miami for $5 million, more than double its value on the NASDAQ stock exchange. He received $1.58 million for his 158,000 shares and stayed on at Norin as Chairman and consultant (The New York Times, Sunday, April 10th, 1977).

Parks was a pragmatic and determined man who is optimistic about the prospects for his race and his adopted city of Baltimore. He believed that real strength of America is in its business and industry. Said Parks, "I think we need to learn how to be managers and how to operate profitable businesses because we will never learn how to be strong as a people until we begin to have self-sufficiency, access to money and the proper use of it."

Other achievements include serving as a member of the Baltimore City Council, President of the Baltimore City Fire Board, and being granted honorary Doctorates from Morgan State University and Temple University.

Charles Shipley (1879-1943) was at the turn of the century, a black man who towered over others in his profession—catering.

Shipley began his business in 1909 and soon rose to international prominence. He was known everywhere by his last name. All major social occasions in Baltimore were catered by Shipley and his associates. He started out serving and preparing the most elaborate private parties. His access behind the scenes to the very well-to-do made him an authority on who's who in society.

Shipley was born in Baltimore in 1879, coming from a line of house servants. His parents were both born on a Howard County, Maryland estate where they were brought up in the tradition of house service. He was educated at St. Catherine's parochial school. At age twelve, he went to Canada and worked as a stable boy. Disenchanted with his experience, Shipley, after two years, took up the family tradition of serving prominent Baltimore socialites in their mansions.

Shipley's Catering arranged commercial and industrial entertainment affairs of high magnitude. But what gave him distinction as an internationally known caterer was the large number of royalty he served. Queen Marie of Romania, Cardinal Mercier of Belgium, Prince Paul of Greece, Cardinal Gibbons of Baltimore, and Britain's celebrated Duke and Duchess of Windsor were some of his ardent admirers. King Prajadhipok proved to be the greatest admirer, having on several occasions arranged shipment of the Shipley specialty, Maryland terrapin, to his royal palace in Spain.

As a businessman, Shipley knew the value of presenting a good image.

John O'Ren of the Sunpaper wrote after his death in March 1943, "If Shipley were given charge of an affair, there was a man to open the door, a man to take your coat, a man to serve cocktails, and another to pass canapes…he could come into any house or apartment and turn it into an evening in some sort of ducal palace."

A lover of "finer things in life" by nature or breeding, Shipley's disposition would allow him to accept the era, which he called, "the gin, jazz, hot dogs, and blues days." He looked with longing back to the times when "…the finest of madieras, canaries, and other rare wines graced Baltimore's dinner tables and gentlemen drank their whisky straight." Shipley died a wealthy man with one well-known virtue: he did well the things he set out to do.

Shipley had two children, Charles Ridgely Shipley, deceased, and Joy Shipley-Cooke. According to Ms. Shipley-Cooke, a ninety-year-old retired principal from New York Public Schools, her father purchased two adjacent houses and lived in one at 708 Madison Avenue, Baltimore city. The second property was used for the kitchen, work room, and office of the business where one would frequently find live Maryland terrapins purchased from Faidley's Seafood at the world-famous Lexington Market. Ms. Shipley-Cooke often observed terrapin, the fashionable delicacy, in her father's kitchen, and admitted her first taste of terrapin came much later while on a date at the 21 Club in New York City, where she had relocated and currently resides.

Nelson Wells (1786 -1843) died eighteen years before the Civil War began. When many of his brethren served as slaves, Wells, a freedman, was building a profitable business as a drayman, or what could be likened to a present-day truck hauler.

By 1832, Wells' business (horse and cart) was worth a whopping $100. He invested in Baltimore municipal stocks, and in real estate, owing property along the Charles Street waterfront. He resided at 2475 Charles Street until his death.

It is reported that Wells laid in in his Charles Street home in a depleted state. Leeches had begun to work their way over his body. His doctor tells that he held his hand and told him that he wanted to make a provision in his Will for the "intellectual improvement of poor free colored children of Baltimore." Two years after his death in 1845, the Wells Free School was established. The school was located on Hanover Street and Cypress Alley, enrolling an average of forty students annually. The 1903 catalogue of the Baltimore Normal School for the Education of Colored Teachers stated that the school received funding from the Wells Trust. The Baltimore Norma School later became Bowie State College.

T. Wallis Lansey (1893-1948) entered into a partnership in 1913 with Henry T. Pratt, then owner and operator of Druid Laundry. Druid Laundry began in 1898 by Pratt to provide employment opportunities for women. Employment elsewhere was virtually non-existent. After the partnership developed, the laundry was moved to 1634 Druid Hill Avenue, where it remained until 1968.

Lansey, an easy-going, independent thinking businessman, employed at one time over seventy persons located throughout the city of Baltimore and counties of Maryland. What enabled him to maintain such a sizable workforce were the lucrative contracts won with the B & O Railroad.

The Druid Laundry provided services for all B & O dining and parlor cars from Jersey City, New Jersey to St. Louis, Missouri. With an additional ten street routes and nine stores to service, the business competed successfully with all laundry companies, both black and white.

Devoting his time to civic, church, and community affairs was a priority of Lansey. He was particularly interested Providence Hospital and served as a member of its board for many years, holding such positions as secretary and president. Lansey was one of the founders of Ideal Savings and Loan Association, and in 1920, was named its president. In 1928, Mayor Broening appointed him to the Board of Supervisors of the Baltimore City Charities. Two years later, he became a member of the advisory Council to the Unemployment Compensation Board, Treasurer of the Maryland Association for the Promotion of Business, and a member of the Frontier Club.

As an active churchman, Lansey was a member of the St. Peter Claver's Catholic Church, the board of the Mission Helpers of the Sacred Heart, and was an affiliate of the Archbishop's Confraternity of the Laity.

In 1917, Lansey married Josephine Gaines; together the two had eight children. One of his sons, Gaines, headed the Ideal Savings and Loan Association on Druid Hill Avenue. Gaines Lansey remembered his father as kind and considerate who was a good provider for the family. Gaines Lansey said of his father, "He was also an engineer and a naturally born tinkerer, always fixing or building things around the house. But in raising his children, he was a stern taskmaster. If you wanted two cents worth of snowball, he'd want two cents worth of work in turn."

Roger Sanders graduated from the Apex & Bonaparte Beauty School in New York City in 1930.

Upon graduation he immediately established his own beauty salon, which he operated until 1955. After twenty-five years in the beauty salon business, Sanders and his wife, Dorothy, moved to Baltimore.

Sanders sold jewelry for a while and later began selling beauty supplies out of his basement. Due to the rapid growth of the business, after one year, he moved from his basement to 1829 Appleton Avenue, and shortly thereafter, to 2424 Pennsylvania Avenue. The number of manufacturer's products grew to over thirty-five, and the number of beauty shops he supplied increased dramatically.

As a supplier, Sanders offered free hair clinics for eight years, touting himself as the first to introduce chemical straighteners and everything new in ethnic hair care, except the wet curl look to Baltimore. During the next twenty-six years, Sanders began manufacturing his own line of products that sold well over 100,000 items. He had market-wide distribution in every drug store and supermarket that carried an ethnic line.

Sanders described his formula for success as "a total positive attitude, time-tabled goals, and professionalism." Describing himself as a total positive person, Sanders advises, "If one desires to survive in business, never dwell on money. If the marketing plan is put together well, the money will come. Planning is a necessity for success," according to Sanders. "If one desires something in life, a plan must be made to bring that desire to fruition. Having something to strive for, make short and long-term plans to get what you want in life." Mr. Sanders often stated that he would also like to see the public-school system implement a mandatory course in attitudes, motivation, and salesmanship. He died March 31, 1998.

1986

Walter T. Dixon (1893-1980) was a pioneering black educator and politician. As a Baltimore resident from the mid-1930s, Dixon was an educator and founding member of the Cortes W. Peters Business School of Baltimore. At a time when other schools were segregated, the Peters Business Schools opened its doors to young blacks entering the business field. Dixon retired as a Dean of his school in 1974 and was one of the first black councilmen elected to the Baltimore City Council in 1955. Representing the Fourth District for three terms, Dixon helped to institute much of the Civil Rights legislation throughout the 1950s and 1960s. He was also a prime mover in the establishment of citywide public accommodations, fair housing, anti-poverty programs, and equal employment opportunities.

Dixon was a graduate of Benedict College in Columbia, South Carolina, the American Institute of Law in Chicago, and Columbia University, where he earned a Bachelor's and a Master's Degree. He also earned a Master's Degree from Howard University and did graduate work at Harvard, Rutgers, and Yale Universities.

Camilla White Sherrard was associated with the Arena Players of Baltimore, a community-based voluntary theater group. Prior to establishing the Playhouse at its current location, at McCulloh Street, the Arena Players had a nomadic existence. Under the leadership of Sherrard, she acquired an old warehouse building and converted it into the current Playhouse.

Through her guidance, more than one million dollars was raised for capital improvements and designed to accommodate a 300-seat semicircular arena on the first level. Second and third levels were renovated to house the Youth Theatre, a group development center for youth, a carpenter's shop, dance studio, art center, and office facilities. Her leadership encouraged the establishment of a board of directors, significant increased fundraising efforts, which helped her to establish the theater, a 501(c) (3), tax exempt, non-profit corporation.

Sherrard implemented an executive management system in all areas of the Arena Player's operation. She was instrumental in the organization to continue as the oldest consistently operating, black-owned theater of its kind in the United States. Sherrard was born in Virginia, moved to Baltimore, where she attended Coppin State College and graduated with honors. She holds a B.S. Degree from Morgan State University, a M.A. degree from New York University, and a D.Ed. degree from Columbia University.

Thomas H. Kerr (1888-1985) is a native of Cambridge, Maryland and was considered a Baltimorean since 1904. As a student of the violin, self-taught musician of piano and flute, Kerr was a composer and famous leader of orchestra. Kerr attended Howard University's School of Pharmacy, and after passing his state board examination, he graduated from Howard in 1912.

He balanced his schedule as a working musician and a registered pharmacist in local drug stores before opening his own drug store in 1919. As a pharmacist, Kerr created a line of sixteen products, of which Kerr's Kell-A-Kough became the most popular for more than fifty years.

Kerrs's Drug Store was sort of a community center where Kerr dispensed advice, along with health remedies. He enthusiastically supported the youth in his community with a unique display of black historical figures in his store. He also frequently assisted elderly residents with explaining their complicated business tax forms. He was the first Baltimorean to purchase an individual life membership in the National Association for the Advancement of Colored People (NAACP). Kerr and his daughter, Louise, were co-plaintiffs in a lawsuit, which they filed against the Enoch Pratt Library for employment discrimination.

"Captain" George W. Brown (No Picture)
Marine Engineer, Navigator, Entrepreneur

George W. Brown ("Captain"), a machinist, steamboat fireman, packer, and laundry employee who came to Baltimore penniless in 1896. By 1927, he had become the wealthiest black man in the city. His treatment as a passenger on a steamboat later motivated him to purchase a steamboat and forty-five acres of land in Anne Arundel County that came to be known as Brown's Grove. Racism, a willingness to work hard, and a determined spirit to overcome adversity were the primary reasons that led many blacks to become entrepreneurs. Such was the case of Captain Brown.

The facts about Captain Brown's life were found in two items printed in the *Evening Sun*. The first was an obituary dated November 27th, 1935. The second was a letter published on October 23rd, 1978, when the Rev. Napoleon Bonaparte Carrington read the newspaper and highlighted Brown's Grove as a favorite amusement park for Negroes in the early 1900s.

It was reported that George W. Brown was born in Little Washington, North Carolina. The date of his birth was not given, but at an early age, Mr. Brown became a machinist. He was such a good machinist that he became the foreman of a machine shop that employed thirty-two white mechanics. Whites apparently resented Brown's position; racial conflicts arose in 1896, and Mr. Brown came to Baltimore penniless. He earned fifty cents for his first night's lodging by helping to unload the steamer on which he had traveled.

He spent the next ten years as a steamboat fireman, a packer, and a laundry employee. It was while working for a laundry that Captain Brown decided to start his own steamboat business. At that time, Captain Brown was sent to the Eastern Shore with several white men to bring some machinery to Baltimore. During his trip, he was forced to ride in the baggage car with a bird dog.

This treatment made him very determined to start a transportation business that would provide first-class accommodations for Negro Travelers.

When Mr. Brown returned to Baltimore, he decided to quit his laundry job and chartered a small steamer for twenty-five cents a day. In 1906, he purchased a boat he called "Dr. J.W. Newbill." That boat had a capacity of 300. Around the same time, Mr. Brown and Walter R. Langley, a black merchant who owned a business in the Broadway Market, purchased forty-five acres of land and established what was referred to as the finest amusement park and picnic grounds in this state, "Brown's Grove."

Local citizens who remembered Brown's Grove described it as a park that was constantly improving. It had picnic pavilions, roller coasters, flying horses, swings, a skating rink, a miniature railroad, boating, bathing beaches, and a dance pavilion to accommodate 500 people. Mr. Brown used his steamer to transport church groups, fraternal organizations, school children, the elite and working men and women to Brown's Grove at a cost of fifty cents round trip fare for adults and twenty-five cents for children.

In 1907, Captain Brown purchased another boat called the "Starlight." It had a capacity of 900 but often had to make more than two trips each day to transport large numbers of passengers headed for Brown's Grove.

In 1912 or 1914 (depending upon the article one selects as a source), the Starlight was burnt while it was docked at Rock Creek, so Captain Brown purchased another steamer called the "Favorite" for $100,000.

An advertisement for Mr. Brown's business enterprises appeared in a 1925 edition of the Afro-American newspapers and described Brown's Grove and the steamer, "Favorite" as follows:

> *"This is the only steamer and the only park in the State of Maryland run exclusively for colored people and by colored people..."*

Captain Brown operated the Favorite until 1928 when he purchased another steamer. That steamer, unfortunately, was caught in a storm off the Jersey Coast while being towed to Baltimore. It was "beached off" Atlantic City, a wreck, with the loss of three crew members, according to one source.

Captain Brown then purchased the "Avalon," which remained in service until 1934 when he became ill and had to give up his command. This steamer carried 1,500 passengers, and he used that steamer to transport passengers from its pier to Brown's Grove and to rescue people during storms.

(*The Avalon* steamship at Secretary, Maryland, on the lower Choptank River). This picture appeared on page 67 of *Steamboats Out of Baltimore*, published January 1st, 1968 by Tidewater Publishers, author Robert H. Burgess.

"During a thirty-year period, Captain Brown and Brown's Grove became an institution. The moonlight excursions from 8 P.M to midnight, down the bay and return, were the "delight" of working men and women. According to one article, *"The steamer schedule was arranged for the convenience of special groups of Negro workers, necessitating its departure and arrival at odd hours of the night and early morning."*

Occasionally, "she" got into trouble and had a breakdown or suffered some other delay, which meant that 1,500 domestics would be late getting to work on Monday morning. Another reporter said, *"The Saturday evening Twilight Excursions were reserved for the elite! They had some musician as Dr. T. Henderson Kerr's orchestra with Professor Ernest Purviance as dancing master. These excursions departed from the wharf at the foot of Broadway."*

According to a former schoolteacher and State Delegate, Lena K. Lee, *"School teachers used Captain Brown's steamer each spring to take children to Brown's Grove. I remember swinging on the swings. As far as I know and can remember, Mr. Brown's steamer and excursion trips to Brown's Grove were not always a profitable enterprise. He donated so much out of love and concern."*

By written accounts and personal recollections, Captain Brown was a respected, intelligent man. He belonged to several fraternal organizations and had numerous other business interests in addition to his excursion boats and amusement park. He was quite active in the National Business League. Whatever his resources, it was reported in the *Baltimore News American* on February 5th, 1927 that *"Captain George W. Brown [is] reputed to be the wealthiest Negro in Baltimore..."*

"...It is said that his vessels have carried 3,500,000 passengers to [Brown's Grove] since it opened."

Captain Brown died November 27, 1935 at the Marine Hospital after being ill for more than a year. His home was located at 2103 Druid Hill Avenue in Baltimore.

Brown's Grove, a popular destination for African Americans, enjoyed its heyday in the 1920s. Captain George Brown conducted steamboat excursions and managed the amusement park along with Mr. Walter L. Langley.
(By Yvonne Davis-Robinson, freelance writer.)

1990

William L. Adams, born January 14th, 1914 in Zebulon, North Carolina.

Long before he came to Baltimore in 1929, Adams knew the value of hard work and ingenuity. Reared by his grandparents, Adams and his sister grew up in Gethsemane, North Carolina. Adam's grandmother, a schoolteacher, instilled love of learning in her grandson. Early, she observed his interest in mathematics. When he was just four, he worked alongside his grandfather, a sharecropper, to earn enough money to buy a coveted bicycle. Adams came to Baltimore at the height of the depression and landed a job in a rag factory. Later he went to work in an East Baltimore bicycle shop. Adams was nicknamed Little Willie by his friends and wanted more out of life than the bicycle shop could offer. On fire with ambition, he used his native wit and intelligence to carve out a niche for himself. Several years later, not long after he arrived in Baltimore, he purchased an East Baltimore row house for $400 at the age of nineteen. That was his first foray into the real estate business.

In 1935, at the age of twenty-one, the up-and-coming entrepreneur ventured into the entertainment business when he purchased a three-story building at the corner of Druid Hill Avenue and Whitelock Street. Little Willie's Inn was one of his first-class taverns for Blacks in the Sugar Hill section of the city. From Sugar Hill, Adams moved into what soon became the black entertainment mecca of the city – Pennsylvania Avenue. The year was 1938. The building was located in the 1500 block of Pennsylvania Avenue, and two years later in 1940, that building became the Club Casino.

Opportunity knocked on his door in 1946 when Henry G. Parks, who was then working for a small Cleveland concern, the Craton Sausage company, convinced Adams to purchase shares in the company. Soon the two of them opened a Baltimore plant at Etting and Wilson Streets, later known as Parks Sausage. It had the famous slogan, "More Parks Sausage, Mom, please?" It was heard in millions of homes. In 1969, the company became the first black-owned public-traded company in the country.

Soon Adams diversified his business and in addition to his Pennsylvania Avenue clubs, he purchased Biddison's, a juke-box company. This entity serviced 300 locations. His business interest included real estate development, beauty parlors, liquor stores, and the Metro Plaza, which was adjoined to the Mondawmin Mall. Adams also financed Super Pride supermarkets, which was headed by Charlie Burns, a cousin of Thurgood Marshall. Adams was known as the venture capitalist and routinely received a percentage from the businesses for which he provided financial assistance.

Coincidently, when the Maryland State Lottery was established in 1973, Adams was hired by the Commission as a consultant. It realized that Adams had a complex and thorough knowledge of business analytics that were necessary to implement and operate. His contributions and those of others were evidenced by the long-standing and successful Maryland State Lottery (Frederic N. Rasmussen and The Baltimore Sun, June 28th, 2011).

Although never a candidate for public office, Adams' support for the minority candidate was legion. His wife, Victorine Q. Adams, was the first black woman to be elected to the Baltimore City Council.

Whether working in the 1950s with Dr. Lillie Carroll Jackson, the mother of Baltimore's Civil Rights Movement, leading boycotts against beer distributorship in the 1940s or founding minority business organizations, like Help Unite Baltimore (HUB) in the 1960s, Adams' commitment to Civil Rights, and to the community, was by any standard impressive. As a tribute to the fact that Adams' business acumen was appreciated beyond the Baltimore region, Morris Brown University awarded him an Honorary Doctorate Degree. He and his wife created the Victorine Q. and William L. Adams Foundation that supported a variety of educational and civic causes. Adams died June 27, 2011.

Harry A. Carpenter born in Baltimore on September 6th, 1885. He was known for having built the New Albert Hall Auditorium. It was done at a time when the black community had no other place to have large dances or other major events. Morgan Sate College (now University) used the auditorium for their home basketball games as did various high schools. Carpenter was among the many promoters who brought big name bands like Cab Calloway and Lionel Hampton to Baltimore. Carpentere died January 24, 2003.

He worked for the Mutual Benefit Society for forty-five years and was a violinist who played both at Union Baptist and Sharpen Leeadenhall Baptist Churches. He played and directed the Commonwealth Band and the Colored Baltimore City Orchester.

The New Albert Hall Auditorium was located across the street from the Northwestern Police Station. The first floor housed a garage, five stores, to include a grocery store, shoe repair shop, barber shop, and a beauty salon. On the second floor were apartments. The hall was able to accommodate up to 1,000 people.

Anthony Thomas (1857-1931) was born on the Eastern Shore of Maryland and came to Baltimore in the 1880s where he worked at Sparrow's Point as a Rigger Foreman.

While working at Bethlehem Steel, he worked in Buffalo, New York and Australia. Thomas and his wife, Annie Green Thomas, had six children and were pioneers in the Turner's Station community, an all-black community that grew from 12,000 to 15,000 persons in the industrialized Southwest Section of Baltimore County. Mr. Thomas was one of the founders of the first building association, Tuxedo Savings and Loan, which helped area pioneers build homes and the St. Matthews A.M.E. Church. He also opened a grocery store and real estate office.

Joseph H. Thomas, M.D. (1885-1963) liked to recall that he received his first practical experience in handling money at his father's store located at Main Avenue and Sollers Point Road. Among the businesses that Dr. Thomas developed at Thomas Corner were Anthony Homes, a twelve-unit housing project, the Anthony Theatre, a store, and his offices.

1992

In 1992, the Black Business Hall of Fame inducted Charles Thurgood Burns (1914-1991), founder and chairman of Hilton Court Pharmacy, Inc. and Super Pride Markets that impacted thousands of people throughout his life. As a young boy, Burns worked in his grandfather's

grocery store and later, while attending Morgan State College, he sold fresh produce and seafood from a wagon.

In the 1930s, Burns went to work for Acme Markets, and in 1935, he became the first chain store manager in Baltimore city. Four years later, he opened his own grocery store at the corner of Madison Avenue and Traction Street. Burns moved to another venture when he became owner and part operator of Club 1017, which was a popular bar and restaurant on Madison Avenue.

In1962, Burns acquired Hilton Court Pharmacy, which eventually grew into a chain of six stores.

In 1969, while contemplating retirement, he was approached by George L. Small, then President of P.A. & S Small Company, a grocery wholesaler based in York, Pennsylvania. Mr. Small wanted Burns to take over the financially-troubled Super Jet Markets, a black run, one-store operation that owed more than $800,000 and was on the verge of bankruptcy. It took Burns almost a year to take the offer.

He was asked to invest $100,000 and replied, *"I'm not smart, but why would I put $100,000 in when you all are experts and lost $800,000?"* Burns offered one dollar for the business, and they accepted it.

Burns changed the name from Super Jet to Supper Pride Markets, and over the next twenty-one years, Super Pride Markets went from one unprofitable store with a handful of employees, to a Baltimore retail food chain, which consisted of seven profitable stores with more than 400 employees. Burns, a native of Baltimore, never forgot his roots. He provided personal scholarships to young gifted black students, counseled many aspiring entrepreneurs, and contributed to various community activities.

Raymond V. Haysbert Sr. (1902-2010), was inducted into the Black Business Hall of Fame. Haysbert had become Chairman, CEO, and majority owner of H.G. Parks, Inc., better known as the Parks Sausage Company, which was head-quartered in Baltimore.

Haysbert joined the company in 1952 after a seven-year tenure on the business instruction faculty at Central State University. After joining Parks Sausage, his efforts had boosted the company's revenues from $700,000 to over $28 million.

He was a native of Cincinnati, Ohio and held a Mathematics degree from Wilberforce University and an Accounting degree from Central State University.

He attended the Johns Hopkins University, the University of Baltimore, and Morgan State University, where he lectured in the School of Business.

In 1988, Haysbert was named Executive of the Year by *Baltimore Magazine*. In September 1991, he was honored at the White House by President Bush with two distinguished awards: the Regional Minority Manufacturer of the Year and National Minority Entrepreneur of the Year.

Haysbert continued to receive numerous awards and citations to include the 1992 Black Engineers Award, a Laureate in the Baltimore Business Hall of Fame by Junior Achievement of Central Maryland, Distinguished Black Marylander, and Outstanding Black Businessman.

As the founder of Advance Federal Savings and Loan, he served on its Advisory Board, as well as the Advisory Board of Harbor Bank of Maryland and Maryland National Bank. Haysbert was Director Emeritus of Bell Atlantic Corporation, the Baltimore Branch of the Federal Reserve Bank of Richmond, and was President Emeritus of the HUB Organization. He received an Honorary degree in Public Services from the University of Maryland and the distinguished honor of being a Civilian Aide to the Secretary of the United States Army in Maryland.

1993

Parren J. Mitchell (April 29th, 1922 – May 28th, 2007) was a retired member of the U.S. House of Representative (D., 7th Cong. Dist.), an acclaimed leader and champion for minority business and economic development. He was a native of Baltimore, Maryland.

Mitchell graduated from Morgan State University and the University of Maryland at College Park. In 1950, he paved the way for future admissions of African Americans and other minorities to the University of Maryland. He successfully sued for admission and became the first black to undertake graduate study at the College Park Campus. Mitchell graduated with a Master's Degree in Sociology with honors in 1952.

Mitchell's dedicated and momentous achievements for the cause of blacks and the poor were numerous. In the 1960s, Mitchell served as Executive Secretary for the Maryland Human Relations Commission, where his diligent work was influential in the enactment and implementation of Maryland's Public Accommodations Law. He also served as Executive Director of the Baltimore City Community Action Agency, where he strongly lobbied the federal government to provide funds for the agency's anti-poverty programs.

In 1970, Mitchell was elected as Maryland's first Black Congressman. In this role, he earnestly sought economic development for minorities through legislation, which compelled state, county, and municipal governments to set aside ten percent of federal funds for legitimate minority firms. Further, in 1978, Public Law 95-507 was enacted after Mitchell introduced legislation, which required contractors to submit provisions for awarding contracts to minority contractors. Due to his reformative legislation, minority businesses had access to proposed business contracts worth billions of dollars. As Chairman of the House Committee on Small Business, Mitchell urged the federal government to establish the Surface Transportation Assistance Act of 1982 and the Surface Transportation and Uniform Relocation Assistance of 1987 to provide for minority participation in highway construction projects.

Upon retirement from Congress, Mitchell founded the Minority Business Enterprise Legal Defense and Education Fund, Inc. (MBELDEF) in 1980 where he later served as Chairman of that Board. MBELDEF provided legal and technical assistance to government concerns, as well as public and private sector programs.

He also served as member and leader of several committees and commissions, which included Whip-At-Large, Senior Member of the House Banking, Finance and Urban Affairs Committee, Chairman of the Subcommittee on Domestic Monetary Policy, Chair of the Task Force on Minority Enterprise, Chairman of the Subcommittee on Housing, Minority Enterprise and Economic Development of the Congressional Black Caucus, Member of the Joint Economic Committee, and Member of the Presidential Commission on the National Agenda for the Eighties. Mitchell received numerous awards, which included fourteen Honorary Degrees.

1994

Allen Quille (August 17th, 1919 – January 1st, 2002) was born in Baltimore, Maryland to Percy and Etta Quille. He attended schools in Baltimore City and Calvert County. Quille's formal schooling ended at age fourteen, and he went to work for a man who owned two parking lots. He was drafted in the U.S. Army where he served until 1946. While in the army, he had the opportunity to display his musical talents and served as Assistant Director of the 213th Army Band. He also served as Supply Sergeant.

Quill returned to Baltimore, where his former employer offered him a fifty-fifty deal if he would run the parking lot. Five decades later, Quille's parking lots were found throughout the Baltimore Metropolitan area. He later merged them with Crown Parking, Inc. to form Quille Crown Parking, Inc.

Quille served as an officer or board member for many local and international organizations. He served as a board member of the Equal Opportunity Commission, the American Red Cross, Boy Scouts and Girl Scouts of America, Better Business Bureau, United Negro College Fund, Liberty Medical Center, Coppin State College, Retinitis Pigmentosa, Democratic National Finance Committee, Advisory Board to the Department of Economic and Community Development, Chair of the Maryland Chapter of the UNCF, Board of Directors of Carrollton Bank, the Awards Board of Directors of Carrollton Bank, the Awards Board for the city of Baltimore, Advisory Board of the University of Maryland, American Israel Society, member of the Signal 13 Foundation, Chairman of the Baltimore Parking Society, and many others.

In 1977, Quille was General Chairman for the NAACP Mississippi Campaign and received honors for raising over $1,650,000, the largest amount raised by any state in the nation. He also volunteered to become Chairmen of Restoration Plus, a program to build a large and improved St. Francis Academy, which was conducted by the Oblate Sisters of Providence, located at 501

E. Chase Street. When it was completed, over $4 million dollars were raised for improvements to the Academy.

In May 1991, Western Maryland College honored him with an Honorary Doctorate Degree for Public Service. He was honored by a host of civic charities, government, and religious institutions. Equally at home with rich and poor, black and white, Jew, or Gentile, all have been recipients of Quille's charity. He was a true champion of causes, a humanitarian who exemplified dedication to mankind through his selfless service.

Kenneth O. Wilson (November 5, 1918- June 17th, 2004) was born in St. Paul Minnesota. He was educated in the elementary and secondary schools of St. Paul and trained at the University of Minnesota's School of Social Work at Minneapolis.

Wilson began his career as a cottage supervisor at the Indiana Boys' School at Plainfield, Indiana. He enlisted in the U. S. Naval Reserve and joined the physical training staff at the Great Lakes Naval Training Center. He later trained more than one million recruits as part of the recruitment program at Great Lakes. After being honorably discharged from the Navy, Wilson returned to St. Paul, Minnesota and became the Boy's Work Secretary at the Hallie Q. Brown Community House at St. Paul, Minnesota.

Wilson joined the Marion, Indiana branch of the of the National Urban League as its Executive Secretary. His career changed from social work to business when he joined the Johnson Publishing Company, publishers of *Ebony, Jet, Ebony Man* and *Ebony Jr.* Wilson resigned from the company in 1957 and formed Kenneth Wilson Associates, a merchandizing consultant organization in Chicago, Illinois.

He later joined the *Afro-American Newspaper* in Baltimore, Washington, Richmond, and Newark. Wilson resigned his position at the *Afro-American Newspaper* as Senior Vice President in 1986 to devote his full-time operating his family business, The Inner Harbor Marina of Baltimore, Inc.

He organized The Dorchester Group, which was a development company, headquartered in Baltimore, Maryland. He served on the following boards in the Baltimore Region: Enoch Pratt Library, Mayor's Council of Business Advisors, Advisory Board of the University of Baltimore,

Yale Gordon College of Liberal Arts, a Director of the Area Council of YMCA's Operation Sail, The Fort Smallwood Marine Institute, and Special Assistant to the Chairman of Orbital Astronomical Observatory. Wilson also served as Chairman of the Board of Metro Democrats, Inc., Chairman of the Board, Morgan State University Foundation, Chairman of the Board of Provident Hospital, Commissioner of Baltimore Zoning and Appeals Board, Commissioner of Baltimore Civic Center, Director, Maryland Institute of Art, Chairman of the Board, Baltimore Mutual Investment Company, Chairman, Central Dodge, Inc. Civilian Aid to Secretary of the Army for Maryland, Advisory Board, National Alliance of Business Man, Executive Committee of the Volunteer Council on Equal Opportunity, Inc., Vice Chairman, Community Action Agency, and President of the President's Roundtable.

Wilson and his wife Genevieve were members of Providence Baptist Church, Inc. in Baltimore City.

1996

Deaver Young Smith Sr., (August 24, 1890 – Janaury 1975) was born and educated in Baltimore city and was known in the business world as a self-made man. He opened the Smith Punch Base Coffee and Tea Company in 1906 located at 1411 Pennsylvania Avenue, during a time when there were few blacks on Pennsylvania Avenue other than those performing menial tasks. He was the third businessman to open a shop on Pennsylvania Avenue (known to the black community as the "Avenue"). His shop was just fifteen feet wide; originally, the streets were paved with cobblestones and the "sidewalks were brick." There were toilets in the back yard.

In 1922, Smith, a community activist, put up $500 to help finance the Royal Theatre, the first black-owned theatre in Baltimore. The Smith Punch Based Coffee and Tea Company was the foundation that enabled Smith, who married Virginia Biggs, to raise a family of six children, all who attended college. This influence was felt not only by his own children but also by his many nieces and nephews. His strong belief was that "one should be decedent first and then educated."

From 1906 to1974, Smith purchased different blends of coffee beans unroasted and roasted them in his own form: light, medium dark, and very dark roasts. These varieties and mixtures of coffees produced an infinite number of blended possibilities. He was known to do the same with tea blends. Hundreds of individuals in Baltimore, Washington, and Northern Virginia became customers in the early days when deliveries were made door-to door from three horse-drawn wagons.

Restaurants that preferred distinctive blends ordered the bulk of the coffee and tea trade from Smith's company. Freshness added as much to the taste as blending as Smith would say. So he delivered coffee and tea blends in small quantities. His example to deliver a quality product inspired many young men to become self-employed.

Smith was the Treasurer of the Union Baptist Church for over forty years and treasurer of the National Business League, founded by Booker T. Washington and one of the founders of the Colored Grocery Association in Baltimore.

Carroll Henry Hynson Sr. was a longtime resident of Annapolis, Maryland and one of its most successful businessmen.

Henson came from meager beginnings as the son of a domestic and sharecropper family. He possessed only a seventh-grade education. Despite his beginnings, Hynson possessed the fortitude to rise above his circumstances.

In 1931, he left Whitman, Maryland, later known as Hynsontown, with only three dollars and headed for the Annapolis area. He worked as a plumber and then as a waiter at Carver Hall. In 1942, he established the Carroll H. Hynson and Son Real Estate and Bail Bonds Company. This made him the first African American to develop a bail bonds business and obtain a real estate broker/appraisals license in the state of Maryland. In the early 1940s, he was also the only African American to hold a U.S. Postal delivery contract. He paved the way for other African Americans to purchase property in Arundel on the Bay by actively selling and negotiating over 80% of the property in that area. He also organized and financed mortgage loans for many African Americans that allowed them to purchase their first homes.

Hynson was an active community and civic leader. He was a member and former trustee of Asbury Methodist Church. He was also the last of the charter members of Frontiers International of Annapolis. He was a life member of the National Association for the Advancement of Colored People (NAACP) and an ex-officio board member of the Severn Bank.

From 1948 to1953, Hynson developed Capital Hill Manor, which made him the first African American to develop a sub-division in Anne Arundel County. He later developed and owned the first shopping center in the Annapolis area. Hynson died January 19, 1994.

1998

Benjamin L. King was inducted into the BMA's Hall of Fame. On June 27th, 1957, King became the first African American to pass the Certified Public Accountant's examination in the state of Maryland. Benny King, as he was known, was born in Washington, D.C. and attended public schools in the city before attending and graduating from Virginia State (College) University in Petersburg, Virginia.

King served in the U.S. Army and was assigned to the U.S. Army's Audit Unit Agency. Following his military service, he did graduate work in Accounting at American University, Washington, D.C. He was later appointed to the Maryland State Board of Public Accountancy in 1969 and became the first African American in the United States to sit on a CPA board. He was subsequently elected as Chairman of that Board. King also served on Maryland's Commission on Uniformity in Legislation and Regulations of the National Association of State Boards of Accountancy. He was instrumental in having Morgan State University to be recognized by the CPA Board that enabled Morgan's students to sit in Maryland for the exam in 1962.

King received the 1975 National Association of Black Accounts Annual Achievement Award for his outstanding services and achievement in the field of Accounting along with other numerous awards for his contributions to the Accounting profession. King was a full-time lecturer at Morgan State University for fourteen years. He taught Government Accounting Systems, Auditing, and Income Tax. His efforts included all aspects of financial management, establishing new procedures and programs, which were designed to improve financial management operations. King is the founder of the King, King and Associates, P.A., a firm owned by his four children: Pamela, Kara, Anthony, and Martin. The firm offered management, advisory services, audited financial statements, reviewed and compiled financial statements, systems design, upgrade and training, internal control studies, management training, staff seminars, financial planning, and tax compliance and defense. King died March 15, 2005.

2000

Roosevelt Nixon (1926 – 1972) was born in Rocky Point, North Carolina. To escape the grinding poverty of his youth, he joined the Navy shortly after the bombing of Pearl Harbor. He was hard working and indefatigable, and after a year, he was promoted to Chief Petty Officer. While in the Navy, he also became a boxer. He fought some of the best boxers in the armed services and went on to become the middleweight champion of the 7th Fleet.

After a distinguished military career with several accommodations and an award for valor, Nixon was honorably discharged from the Navy in 1946. He was faced with the prospects of returning to the family farm with its painful memories of poverty, racism, or heading North, where greater opportunities beckoned. He chose to settle in Baltimore. Roosevelt's ambition and industry quickly became apparent. He operated a motor pool for a limousine service. At night he rented out the limousine for gypsy cab service in the black community. He also boxed professionally and was immensely proud of having prudently invested every penny of his fight earnings into real estate and other business ventures.

In 1948, Nixon met his wife, Mildred, and the two were married a year later. His wife proved to be a good supporter and able partner whose interest in real estate, particularly farmland, proved to be prophetic. This was especially true at a time when most African American entrepreneurs believed their fortunes were to be made in urban areas.

In 1950, Nixon purchased a small grocery store on Pennsylvania Avenue. He was dissatisfied with the service he was receiving from his landlord, so he bought the building. Eventually, he owned most of the buildings on the block and renovated each one. By 1972, he owned thirteen grocery stores in Baltimore city.

In 1952, Nixon, at the urging of his wife, purchased farmland in Howard County, Maryland. The Nixon's Farm was originally a traditional farm with livestock, silage, and produce, but fate and the ugly vestiges of segregation soon changed that.

In the 1905's, Nixon was one of the founders of the Small Business League, a group of African American and Jewish businessmen who, because of their races or religion, had been denied membership in other business associations.

There were few, if any, large open venues for African Americans. Most places were segregated or restricted. It was during that time that some of his business associates, both African American and Jewish, urged him to create a recreational facility for their families to use. As a result, Nixon's Farm became a favorite site for corporations, private groups, and families to hold their events. The Small Business League's Annual Bull Roast used it to attract some 3,500 attendees. It was also necessary for any politician who wanted to see and be seen by African American voters to use it.

In addition to his business pursuits, Nixon was an active member of Shiloh Baptist Church where he was a deacon. He was a philanthropist who contributed to many charities and individuals. He was active in the Republican Party and believed that African Americans should not be held hostage to adhering to one political affiliation.

Nixon was killed on November 22nd, 1972 during a robbery attempt at his Bond Street grocery store while trying to protect his employees. He left a legacy of hard work, community service, and love for his family.

Nixon's Farm developed into a diversified company, which offered banquet facilities, indoor and outdoor meeting spaces, wedding facilities, destination and meeting planning, on and off-site catering, intuitional food service, and senior assisted living.

2004

Reginald F. Lewis (December 7, 1942 -January 19, 1993) a product of Baltimore, attended the renowned Paul Lawrence Dunbar High School. He played football, basketball, and baseball where he was named captain of each sport. He graduated from Virginia State University

and later from Harvard Law School. Upon graduating from Harvard in 1968, Lewis worked for the prestigious law firm, Paul & Weiss. Within two years, he established his own Wall Street firm, helping many minority businesses obtain badly-needed capital, and used Minority Enterprise Small Business Investment Companies.

With a desire, as he often said to "do deals myself," he started the TLC Group, L.P. in 1983. His first major deal was the $22.5 million leverage buyout of the McCall Pattern Company. Lewis nursed the struggling company back to health.

Black Enterprise Magazine reported in its November 1987 issue that Lewis purchased the international division of Beatrice Foods, with holdings in thirty-one countries, for $985 million, which became known as TLC Beatrice International. This deal was the largest-leveraged buyout ever of overseas assets by an American company. In 1992, the company had sales of over $1.8 billion. Lewis then created the Reginald F. Lewis Foundation, where he made grants of approximately $10 million to the following: $1 million to Howard University and $3 million to Harvard Law School. This was, at the time, the largest grant in history to the law school. Lewis' remarkable career was cut short by his untimely death at the age of fifty in January 1993 after a short illness.

He said one day that he was going to be a millionaire. *"Why should white guys have all the fun?"* *Reginal F. Lewis & Blair S. Lee, p 40.*

Eddie C. Brown was born in Apopka, Florida in1940 to a thirteen-year-old mother. He had

overwhelming odds stacked against him but managed to overcome those circumstances and became the pinnacle of success, among the top 1% of the nation's wealthiest Americans – a centi-millionaire by some estimates.

From a pre-teen moonshine runner in Central Florida to founder of Brown Capital Management, a Baltimore investment firm with more than $12 billion in assets under management, Brown from an early age believed that he would beat the odds. Brown's employees own the firm, seventy percent of whom are minorities.

Brown's entrepreneurial leanings were acquired from his Uncle Jake, who had his hand in everything from moonshining to migrant labor contracting. This taught him the value of personal initiative early in life and gave him a dogged desire to become the master of his own financial destiny. Brown's confidence and good nature came from the steady hand and loving heart of his grandmother, Mamie Magdalene Brown. She profoundly believed in her grandson's promise.

Brown graduated from high school at sixteen, and his journey began with his entrance into Howard University where he met Sylvia Thurston, his foundational support. Their shared values and collaborative relationship sustained Brown through life's trials and launched his meteoric rise to prominence. After graduation Brown was offered and accepted a position at Martin Marrietta as an electrical engineer. He was later offered and accepted a position as an electrical engineer at IBM. During his tenure with IBM, he received his Master's Degree in Business Administration from Indiana University. In 1970, Brown accepted another position with Irwin Management as an equity's analyst. It was there that he once said he found nothing in his professional career *more scintillating and gratifying than dealing with marketable securities.*

In 1973, T. Rowe Price offered Brown the position as Growth-Stock Fund Manager. This was an opportunity with a larger client base than that of Irwin Management. He accepted the position because of T. Rowe Price's commitment to the theory of growth management investments. Brown later spent nine years at T. Rowe Price, a giant global investment firm. In 1983, Brown evaluated his knowledge, skills, business successes, and the increased profitability he brought with him from two firms where he previously worked, and concluded, *"I can definitely do this for myself and do it well."* His first day of business as Brown Capital Management was Tuesday, July 5th, 1983.

Brown quickly became known as the first African American investment celebrity because he was a regular participant with the colorful Louis Rukeyser on the iconic weekly PBS show, *Wall Street Week with Louis Rukeyser.*

Geraldine Whittington, then President Lyndon Johnson's secretary, was a regularly viewer the Louis Rukeyser PBS show. She judged Brown's demeanor as dependable and trustworthy. Fortuitously, when Brown Capital opened its doors for business, she was its first client. Whittington invested with Brown $200,000 from a medical settlement she received.

His financial celebrity success did not deter Brown from another life-long ambition to share his financial success with others in many ways. He was inspired by his anonymous benefactor, a white woman from Allentown, Pennsylvania, who paid his tuition for four years at Howard University. Brown never forgot the value of that generosity. Brown, who never met the "wonderful woman," fondly referred to her as Lady B….B is for benefactor.[1]

It's axiomatic that Brown's growth theory of investment was well-known among the investment community throughout the country. Brown and his wife Sylvia's most enduring legacy perhaps would have the greatest impact on communities throughout central Maryland with their extraordinary generosity. Gifts flowing from The Eddie C. and C Sylvia Brown Family Foundation, easily placed the foundation as an "elite philanthropy" in central Maryland.

Eddie and Sylvia are revered as "remarkably quiet" philanthropists. Without seeking recognition or calling attention to themselves, the Eddie C and C Sylvia Brown Family Foundation, since its inception in 1994 contributed over $39 million to a broad range of causes focusing largely on education and the arts in Baltimore. Much of the foundation's focuses were based on the Browns' strong belief that both education and art "are vital to enabling inner-city youngsters to grow into well-rounded and successful adults who would become assets to their community." Brown's daughters, Tonya and Jennifer, are integrally involved in the distribution decisions of their foundation.

---

[1] *Walker, B.S. (2011) Beating the Odds. Hoboken, New Jersey: John Wiley & Sons, Inc.*

The Roster of Members and Supporters

Abkemeier	Peggy M.	Arthur Andersen LLP
Abram	Nicholas	American Expresss Financial Advisor, Inc.
Abrams	Gerald G.	Abrams, Foster, Nole & Williams
Adams	Sandra	Sahara Publications
Addison	Eric T.	The Business Travel Centre
Alexander	Marcellus	WJZ-TV
Alford	Howard	Morgan State University
Allen	Maxine P.	Contract Brokerage Corporation
Allison	Edwin	Allegheny Pepsi Cola
Anderson Jr	Calvin	U.S. Department of Health and Human Services
Anderson	Tanesha	Baltimore Business Journal
Andrews	Earl M.	American Expresss Financial Advisor, Inc.
Andrus	Tracine	Black & Decker Corporation
Anthony	F.Daryl	Prudential Financial Services, Inc.
Apple	Terry	The Development Council
Archer Sr	Jereleigh	Equitable Bank, N.A.
Archer	Marilyh M.	Cameo Electronics Co., Inc.
Arthur	Jacqueline E.	AFLAC Insurance Company
Asemota	Henry	Legg Mason, Inc
Aston	Joseph L.	Harbor Bank of Maryland
Aston	Tess Hill	Commission on Aging and Retirement Education
Austin	Raymond P.	The Match Group
Austin	Michael	Alex Brown & Sons
Badham	Portia	Liberty Medical Center
Bailey, Jr.	Frederick A.	Maryland National Bank
Baker	Vanessa	Vanita Enterprises
Baldwin	Tina L.	Vision Concepts
Ballard	Ursula L.	USF&G
Banks	Anndell B.	Development Credit Fund, Inc.
Barner	Kay F.	Kay Barner & Associates
Barnhill	Matthew C.	Procter & Gamble
Barnhill, Jr.	Linda A.	J.H. Filbert Inc.
Barrer	Kay F.	KB Associates

Barrett	Saundra V.	SVB Associates
Belizaire	Savitri	University of Maryland Medical Center
Bell	Craig A.	Law Offices of Peter G. Angelos
Bell	Monique L.	Prometric
Best	Elizabeth I.	Best Writing & Consulting Services, Inc.
Bhatti	Maryam A.	Mercantile Safe-Deposit & Trust Company
Biggs	Olivia	Superlative Sales & Marketing
Biggs	Yolanda Y.	Abrams, Foster, Nole & Williams
Billups	Victor D.	The First Financial Group
Black	Thelma	Northwood Transportation
Blake	Charles	Baltimore Gas & Electric Company
Blanheim	Melvin L.	Howard Security Assembly, Inc.
Bobbitt	Hugh	Amoco Oil Company
Bolden	Rosa	Lumbard Middle School
Bollin	Lois	Century 21 Home Specialists
Booker	Monique K.	SB & Company
Boone	Jean Patterson	Baltimore Symphony Orchestra Inc.
Boone	Maurice L.	Boone Interiors
Bornett	Lillian A	Social Security Administration
Boston	Carol A.	Hyatt Regency
Boyd	Darric N.	Legg Mason, Inc
Bradley	Peggy C.	Capital Services Management
Braggs	Gladys W.	Specialty Marketing Printing Service
Branson Jr	Milton R.	Baltimore Gas & Electric Company
Branson	Cassandra	The Food Service Group
Bratton	Patricia	Baltimore Minority Business Development Center
Bravo	Edna J.R.	The Harbor Bank of Maryland
Bravo, Sr.	Earl W.	Chapman Capital Management Inc.
Bravo-Wing	Carla	Java Journey Coffee Company
Braxton	Natalie E.	Development Credit Fund Inc.
Brazile	Kay B.	Midtown Liquors & Deli
Breiner	James	The Baltimore Business Journal
Bridges	Myra	Waverly Press
Briggs	Patricia J.	Maryland Commission of Correctional Services
Brison	Kevin H.	Boy Scouts of America
Britton	Jerry	Legg Mason, Inc
Brook	Benjamin	Joseph E. Seagrams & Sons
Brooks	Ashley	Consultant
Brooks	Janice	Prudential Financial Services
Brooks	Teaira	DEWALT Power Tools & Accessories
Brooks	Valerie	USF&G Company
Brown	June	NVR Mortgage Company
Brown	Bruce G.	Bruce G. Brown Belvedere Valet

Brown	Charlene D.	Joseph H. Brown, Jr. Funeral Home
Brown	Conrad	Westinghouse Electric Corporation
Brown	Edith G.	Ofegro, Inc.
Brown	Jestine	Northern Senior High School
Brown	Jonathan K.	Entrepreneurial Management Services
Brown	June	Crestar Corporation
Brown	Lee	McCormick and Co.
Brown	Michael A.	Brown & Sheehan, LLP
Brown	Michelle R.	Video Production Service Coppin State College
Brown, Esq.	Arnold L.	Allstate Financial Corporation
Bryan	Myra Y.	USF&G Company
Bryant	Joseph L.	Bell Atlantic of MD
Bryant	Louis	Prudential Financial Services
Bryant, Sr.	William	American Graphic Systems
Burgess	Donald	HTMS, Inc
Burnett	Aaron G.	Fidelity & Deposit Co. of Maryland
Burnett	Anne	The Daily Record Company
Burnett	Lillian A.	Social Security Administration
Burton	Kermit C.	The Baltimore Sun
Bush	Kim L.	Greyhound Lines, Inc.
Butler	Octavia E.	The Harbor Bank of Maryland
Butler	Sheila	WJZ-TV 13
Byers	Hilbert	Maryland National Bank
Camp	William	City Bookkeeping Services
Campbell	Lawrence	Westinghouse Electric Corporation
Canion	Barbara A.	Ann Browne & Associates
Carey	Thomas A.	Blue Cross/Blue Shield
Carroll	Rochelle R.	Rouse Co./Mondawmin Mall
Carter	Fredric G.	Waverly, Inc.
Carter	Karence	January & Associates
Carter	Lisa	Pharmeceuticals Corporation
Cassell	Michael	Creative Real Estate Services, Inc.
Cassell, CRB, CRS, GRI	Charles	Attorney at Law
Charles	Gerald T.	Global Technology Corporation
Charles	Lenora D.	Global Technology Corportation
Chester	Frank G.	FMC Corporation
Chester	Cherrilyn D.	Prudential Financial Services
Clark	Daniel E.	C & P Telephone Company of MD
Clark	Michael	Mann & Clark Law Offices
Clarkons, Jr.	Portia	Baltimore City Dept. of Recreation & Parks
Clarkson	Alvin V.	Vision Concepts
Clemons	Michael I.	Landmark Marketing Inc
Close	Hari P.	Sheraton Inner Harbor Hotel

Coakley	Frank B.	Maryland Department of Housing & Community Development
Coates	Norwood T.	Century 21-Associated Real Estate
Code	Brenda Green	Baltimore Gas Electric Company
Cole Jr.	Ralph J.	Beretta (USA) Corporation
Connor-white	Sandra	C & P Telephone Company
Cook	Angela Moore	Development Credit Fund, Inc.
Cooper	Patricia S.	Federal Express Corporation
Cooper	Skyler G.	Campaign Worker
Cottman	Irys J.	Bell South Corporation
Cox	Reginald	Huffard Animal Hospital
Craig	Derrick	Southern Energy Corporation
Crews	Reginald A.	Sun Life Insurance Company
Crowder	Ruth	Student
Cullings	Paula B.	City of Baltimore
Dacres	Chester M.	DACCO SCI, INC.
Dacres, Dr.	Thelma	Baltimore Urban League
Daniel	Lenore	Kelly Services
Daniels	Ted H.	Westinghouse Electric Corporation
Dates	Jannette L.	Coppin State College
Dates	Victor H.	Baker, Watts & Company
Davis	Kimberly	USF&G Company
Davis	Angela	Citicorp Financial, Inc.
Davis	Ovetta M.	Maryland Department of General Services
Deal	Samuel	Harbor Bank of Maryland
Dean	Thomas	East Baltimore Medical Plan
DeJesus	Cynthia T.	Maryland Department of Health and Mental Hygiene
Dejesus, M.Ed.	Earl S.	Bd. Fundamental Ed.
Delaveaux	Velma J.	Allied Capital Research Associates, Inc.
Delaveaux, Dr.	Vashti	Bell Atlantic Management Services, Inc
Dennis	Jacqueline	Silver Spring/Bethesda Ride-On
Dixon	Richard	Merrill, Lynch, Pierce, Fenner & Smith, Inc.
Dixon	Stephanie	The Harbor Bank of Maryland
Dolores West	Delores	The Baltimore Sun
Dorsey Esq.	Emerson	Weinberg and Green
Dorsey, DVM	Tovah I.	Friendship Hospital for Aninals
Dotson	Ileen	Citicorp Financial, Inc.
Douyon	Guy	Pacific Mutual Insurance Company
Dowling	Brian G.	Safeway Stores Inc.— Eastern Div.
Draper	Frances M.	The Afro-American Newspaper Group
Duncan	Shirley	Park Hill Day Care Center
Dunn-Hunt	Stephanie	Dunn & Associates
Earl	Barbara J.	C & P Telephone Company of Maryland
East	Sandra	U.S. Customs Service

Edmondson	John E.	Reliable Liquor Company
Edwards	Lawanda	Warfield's Business Record
Effie	Reynolds	Maryland Parole Commission
Eggleston	Mycale	AFLAC, Inc
Elam	David K. Sr.	FannieMae - Southeast Region
Eley	Earnest	State of Maryland Division of Parole and Probation
Eley	Sheila M.	Internal Revenue Service
Eley, Jr.	Carol Boston	Brookshire Hotel
Ellis	Torin	Method 1518
Ellis	Shina	Residential Tite & Escrow Co.
Ellis	Thomas	Commercial Credit Corp.
Evans	Patray	Prudential Preferred Financial Service
Evans	Serita	Brown & Sheehan, LLP
Everett	B. Yvonne O.	C & P Telephone Company of MD
Ewell	Ava S.	Maryland National Corporation
Fant	Michelle	Youth for Understanding
Fantt	Zerita	C & P Telephone Co.
Felton	Henry D.	Commercial Credit Co.
Fernandez	Sergio	Black & Decker Corporation
Fields	James H.	Miles & Stockbridge
Fitts, III	Joseph H.	The Wharton School
Flowers	Willie	The John Henry Group, LLC
Foster	Annette	Batesville Casket Co.
Franklin	Carl A.	Morgan State College
Franklin, Dr.	Neva W.	C&P Telephone Company of D.C.
Franze	Edwin	The Baltimore Sun
Frazier	Wayne	The Harbor Bank of Maryland
Frederick	Pamela	Westinghouse Electric Corporation
Freeman	Ronald J.	Bowie State University
Freeman	Teressa Y.	Development Credit Fund, Inc.
Fresnel	Jean-Claude Jr.	AFLAC Insurance Company
Frye	Yvonne	Special Promotions by Yvonne
Fulton	Lisa	The Avenue Market
Gaines	Michael A.	Council for Equal Business Opportunity
Galling	James E.	United Funding Corporation
Garlic	Calvin L.	First National Bank of Maryland
Garner	Henry	AFLAC, Inc.
Garner, Jr.	Edward	Charles Center
Garrett, Jr.	Dennis	Baltimore, Inc.
Gatewood, PhD.	Wallace L.	Coppin State College
Gatling	James	United Funding Corporation
Gervais	Michael	American Skyline Insurance Company
Gibson	Kweli	Our World News

Gillis	Jean	Keane, Inc.
Ginyard	Robert G.	The Harbor Bank of Maryland
Givens-Redd	Marie	Baltimore Urban League
Glasco	John A.	Citicorp Financial, Inc.
Goel	Venod	Bowie State College
Goines	Thomas K.	Gist Enterprises Inc.
Golder	Edwin R.	Bowie State University
Gordon	Wendy	Mondawmin Mall/Rouse Company
Graham	Earnest	Get The Message, Inc
Graham	Michael A.	Graham Communications
Graham	Wallace	McCormick & Co.
Grant	J. P.	Chesapeake Business Systems, Inc.
Grant, Esq.	Frederick C.	Attorney-at-Law
Gray	Jacqueline D.	Westinghouse Electric Corporation
Gray	Jo Ellen	Allied-Signal Inc
Gray	Arthur	Baltimore City Dept. of Housing & Community Development.
Green	Giselle L.	Nabisco Brands, Incorporated
Green	Gwendolyn	Baltimore City Health Department
Green	Lucille W.	Baltimore Urban League
Green	William L.	Maryland Industrial Development Financing Authority
Greene	Richard G.	Baltimore, Department of Finance
Greenidge	Clarence	Council for Equal Business Opportunity
Greer	Catrice	Photographer
Gregory	Thomas	First National Bank
Gregory	Tom	Coca-Cola Company
Griffin	Dale V.	Walters Art Museum
Griffin	Gloria A.	Coppin State University
Grims	Gerald	Baltimore Urban League Inc.
Gtascoe	Betty J.	University of MD - Baltimore County
Guy	Jeane C.	Baltimore County Government
Hall	Tina	Lorne Enterprises
Hardnett	Carolyn	Hardnett Communications/EMERGE Magazine
Hargrave, Jr.	John A.	Baltimore G & E Co.
Hargrett	Michael A.	Waverly Inc./Williams and Wilkins Publishers
Harker	Toni	Bay College of Md.
Harley, LMSW, MBA	Ebony M.	CareFirst Blue Cross Blue Shield
Harris	Damion W.	Damion Dot, LLC
Harris	Harvey	Harvey Harris Contractors, Inc.
Harris	Arlinda	Arlinda's Skin & Body Care Salon
Harris	Calvin	
Harris	Damion	Damion Dot, LLC
Harris	Darlene	Council for Equal Business Opportunity
Harris	Deborah H.	Colton's Food, Inc.

Harrison	Annette	Maryland National Bank
Harrison, Esq.	Linda G.	Crestar Bank
Harvey	Ronald	Mondawmin Mall
Hash	Bert	Municipal Employees Credit Union
Hash, Jr.	Ralph E.	Crestar Securities Corporation
Haskins	Joseph L.	Harbor Bank Of Maryland
Haskins	Kim Y.	NAACP
Hawkins	Ramona M.	FannieMae
Hayes	Margaret	University of Maryland School of Pharmacy
Hayes, M.S.	Carl L.	Damon Construction Company, Inc.
Haysbert	Reginald	H.G. Parks, Inc.
Hendericks	Tyricia K.	Consultant
Henderson	Marie	Marie Henderson Enterprises
Hendricks	Tyrica	
Henry	Karen B.	Millenium Community Outreach Institute, Inc.
Henson	Dana	The Henson Company
Henson	Daniel P. III	The Henson Company
Henson	Roland	Grand P. Telephone Co.
Hernandez	Teodoro	Holton Enterprises, Inc.
Herring	Jefferson D.	W. R. Grace
Hines	Betty	American Skyline Insurance Company
Holland	Linda	Boyle-Midway
Holliday	Lauretta A.	USF&G Company
Holly	Zerita	Commercial Credit Corporation
Holmes	Ralph W.	Humble Oil Co.
Holmes	Theodore N.	Atlantic Personnel, Inc.
Holton	Helen	Resource One Management Group
Holton	Hiram	Holton Enterprises, Inc.
Horne	Donna L.	The Chapman Company
Howard	Linda M.	Schaller-Anderson of Maryland
Howze	Lenora	The Baltimore Sun
Huddleston	Gloria J.	Millennium Community Outreach Institute, Inc.
Hunter-Bollin	Lois	Century 21 Home Specialists
Hutley	Doretha	Comptroller's Office, State of Maryland
Hynson	Carroll	PJC & Associates
Incan	Shirley	Park Hill Day Care Center
Irons	Ocie J.	Peterson, Howell & Heather, Inc
Isacoff, Esq.	Richard I.	Provident Bank of Maryland
Jackman	David	First Vehicle Services
Jackson	Gerald	Office Products Co.
Jackson	Henry O.	Chesapeake Securities
Jackson	Jackie D.	Harbor Financial Services
Jackson	Kia A.	M.G.H.

Jackson, Sr.	Troy	Constant Care Medical Center
Jackson-Crute	LaVesta M.	Arthur Andersen LLP
Jackson-Crute	Peggy	PJC & Associates
James	Breiner	The Baltimore Business Journal
Jenell-Trigg	S.	WJZ-TV
Jenkins	Kelvin	Mid-Atlantic Marketing Consultants
Jenkins	Edwina J.	Consultant
Joe	Issac	Attorney At Law
Joe, Jr.	Joel Alan	Harbor Bank of Maryland
Johnson	Derrick	American Skyline Insurance Company
Johnson	Edward S.	Blue Cross/Blue Shield of MD
Johnson	Torrie C.	Plain & Fancy Caterers
Johnson	Wendy-Jo L.	RJR Sales Company
Johnson	Barbara	C & P Telephone Co.
Johnson	Harry W.	Blue Cross/Blue Shield
Johnson	James	Radio One
Johnson	James E.	Webb Radio
Johnson	Ramona N.	FannieMae
Johnson	Richard V.	Attorney At Law
Johnson	Weldon R.	Student - Morgan State University
Johnson, Jr.	David J.	Chamber of Commerce
Jones	Alvin	Holton, Jones & Associates, Inc.
Jones	Elliott C.	Transit Executive
Jones	Andrea M.	Consultant
Jones	Clarence C.	Roger's Beauty Supply Company
Jones	Clarice	Signet Bank
Jones	Doris V.	Heritage United Church of Christ
Jones	Gwendolyn Wynn	Wynn Real Estate Services
Jones	Michael	TBC
Jones	Ophelia	Baltimore Urban League, Inc.
Jordan	Herbert	State of Maryland Governor's Office of Minority Affairs
Jude	George L.	Afro-American Newspaper
Julien	Victor	Madera Wine Co.
Kazem	Fatia	Consultant
Kazem, Dr.	F. Bernard	John Short & Associates
Kennedy	Joe D.	Atlantic Personnel Services, Inc.
Kimbro	George	Vanita Enterprises
King, Esq.	Shelby A. Tucker	Brown & Sheehan LLP
King, Esq.	Alethia C.	Johns Hopkins University
Knight	Mae	Consultant
Knight	Monique S.	Arthur Anderson LLP
Knox	Barbara	Blue Cross/Blue Shield of Maryland
Lake	Moses O.	Consultant

Lamberson	Eric	Hewlett-Packard Corporation
Laney	Queen	Edgewood Management Corp.
Lang	Gerald B.	Prudential Urban Marketing Ofc.
Lansey	Patrick O.	Atlantic Federal Saving & Loan Association
Lashley	Delores	Rouse Company
Lawson	Sheila	Harbor Bank of Maryland
Lawson	Quentin R.	National Alliance of Black School Educators
Lee	Dale G.	Amernican Oil Company
Leggett	Malcom	Allstate Insurance Company
Lewis	Benjamin H.	Abrams, Foster, Nole & Williams
Lewis	Danice	Chase Bank of Maryland
Lewis	Lois M.	The Rouse Corporation
Lewis	Matthew	Consultant
Lewis,III	Gregory K. Sr.	Long & Foster
Lias-Booker, Esq.	Ava E.	Weinberg and Green
Lloyd	Rodney J.	The Food Service Group, Inc.
Lucas	Edward W.	Allied Chemical Co.
Mackie	Tim	Empower Baltimore
Madison	Michelle H.	Maryland National Bank
Majev, Esq.	Howard R.	Weinberg and Green
Maker	Charles	Consultant
Mallory	Irving	The Harbor Bank of Maryland
Mann	Charles E.	Encore Productions, Inc.
Marshall	Dana E.	Abrams, Foster, Nole & Williams
Marshall	Howard	McCormick & Co.
Martin	Earl	The Jason Dennis Company
Mason	Ben	Council for Equal Business Opportunity
Mason	Gloria Gettis	Care First, LLC
Mason	Mildred A.	Roger's Beauty Supply
Massey	Garnetta	The Harbor Bank of Maryland
Maxsam	Felicia	Senior Accountant
McBride	Helene E.	Levindale Hebrew Geriatric Center & Hospital
McBride, Esq.	Portia L.	Maryland National Bank
McBridge	Lois A.F. Esq.	Wright, Constable & Skeen
McClain	Angie	Dept. Parole and Probation
McCloud	Elaine	Delta Business Supplies
McCormick	Nancy E.	Congressman Kweisi Mfume Office
McCrimmon	Penny L.	P. McCrimmon & Associates
McDermott, MSA	Delmore	MaestroQA
McDonald	Glen A.	LeBlanc-Dick Communications
McDougald	Sharon	Housing Opportunities Commission
McDuffy	Sheppard	Brass, Bridge and Associates
McGloutten, Jr.	Robert	Maryland Department of Economic

and Community Development

McIntyre	James C.	Arthur Andersen LLP
McIntyre, Jr.	Almie	PHH Fleet America
McKee	Leroy L.	Sheladia Associates, Inc.
McKelvin	Patricia	The Harbor Bank of Maryland
McKenzie	Stanley	Personnel Pool, Inc.
McKenzie	Isaiah	First National Bank
McKnight	James H.	Palladium, Inc.
Mcneill	Yvonne	Consultant
Meacham	Patricia	EMERGE Magazine
Megginson	Alma	Baltimore Tourism Assoc.
Merritt	Patricia M.	Harbor Bank of Maryland
Miller	Dorothy	Neighborhood Transportation, Inc.
Miller	Lori C.	University of Maryland Medical Systems
Mills	Charles K.	American Type Culture Collection
Minor	Brenda A.	Millenium Community Outreach Inst.Inc.
Minter	James	Consultant
Moody	Carolyn	M & M Management Company
Moody	Brian	Our World News
Moore	Hayden	Watkins Security Agency
Moore	Gwendolyn	Commercial Credit Corporation
Moore	Ovetta	State of Maryland Dept. of Business Development
Moore	Wendy P.	United Negro College Fund, Inc.
Moore, Jr.	Willie S.	Roger's Beauty Supply
Morange	Donald C.	Internal Revenue Service
Morton	Romeka A.	Student
Mosby	Ernest W	Maryland Department of Natural Resources
Mosley	James	Consultant
Muldrow	Quince D.	Network Solutions, Inc.
Muldrow, II	Ackneil M.	Development Credit Fund, Inc.
Murray	Janese F.	AAI Corporation
Naughton	Brian	Producers Video Corporation
Nelson	Erick C.	Roger's Supply Company
Newman	Jay	WJZ-TV 13
Nicholson	Desmond	Citicorp Financial, Inc.
Nunley	Frederick	Dundalk Community College
O'Connor	Estelle	Roasters on the Hill
O'Connor	Kevin	Roasters on the Hill
Olaoye	Olu	Council of Economic Business Oppostunity
Oliver	Kenneth N.	Development Credit Fund, Inc.
O'Neil	Kevin C.	Consultant
Otradovec	Susan	WJZ TV
Owens	Charles	Minority Supplier Development Council

Owen-Smith	Rhonda	The Baltimore Sun
Owes	Lawrence	Procter and Gamble Co.
Palmer	Tammi	Univ of Maryland
Parker	P. Kweku	Carteret Mortgage Corporation
Parker	Anthony	WJZ-TV 13
Parker	Claude	Joseph E. Seagrams & Sons
Parker	Holly M.	WJZ-TV 13
Parrish	Aleta	Baltimore City Community College
Patterson	Gina	Minority Supplier Development Council
Perin	Oliver	Commercial Credit Corporation
Peterson	Arthur E.	Baltimore Minority Business Development Center
Phillips	Curtis A.	O/E Mid-Atlantic
Phillips	Michele	W.B. Doner & Company
Phillips	Sheila. M.	Internal Revenue Service
Pinder	Sharon R.	State of Maryland Governor's Office of Minority Affairs
Pinderhughes Esq.	Alice G.	Alice G. Pinderhughes P.A.
Pinnick	Barbara	Neighborhood Transportation, Inc.
Pollard	Shirley	Linkage, Inc.
Pompey	Alexis R.	Ideal Savings & Loan Association
Pruden	Joshua L.	Baltimore City Public Schools
Pruitt	Robert	Consultant
Pryor	Malcom	The Wharton School
Pugh	Catherine Elizabeth	Strayer Business College
Pumphrey	Denise	Citicorp Financial, Inc.
Purnell	Barry	Union Trust Company
Qualls	Tyrone	Qualls Office Furniture
Quarles, Jr	Robert L.	Greater Baltimore Committee
Queen	James	AT&T Teleconference Services
Rahman	Malik	Governor's Office of Minority Business
Rainey	Yolanda M.	Rainey Day Taylor Made Productions
Randall	Alethia	Johns Hopkins University
Randall	Shirley	Comptroller's Office, State of Maryland
Rasbury	Isaiah	Joseph E. Seagrams & Sons
Reed	Keith	The Baltimore Business Journal
Reed	Sherry L.	Waverly Press, Inc.
Reese	Phyllis	WJZ-TV
Reid	LaVonne	Government of the District of Columbia
Reid	Sina M.	A Touch of Class, Ltd.
Reynolds	Effie	Maryland Parole Commission
Reynolds	Gary	Coppin State College
Rich	John	Maryland Cup Corporation
Richardson	AkIdr	Consultant
Richardson	Audrey	Consultant

Richburg	Shelia A.	University of Maryland Joint Institute
Ridgley	Josephine	Metropolitan Life Insurance Company
Roach	Kia A.	Harbor Bank
Roberson	Joshua	Brown & Roberson Associates, Inc.
Roberts	James L.	Coppin State College
Roberts	Nathalia	Balto City Public Schools
Robinson	Yvonne Davis	The Baltimore Sun
Robinson	Carolyn	The New Daily Record
Robinson	Charles T.	Kwik Kopy Business Center
Robinson	Florine	MIS Support, Stop Shop & Save/Baines Mgmt.
Robinson, Sr.	Jean Smith	Smith Temporaries
Ross	William	Council for Equal Business Opportunity
Rossello	Patrick M.	Deloitte Haskins & Sells
Ruffin, Esq.	Rodney P.	Weinberg and Green
Ryles	Clifford	Ambassador Travel, Inc.
Sands	Freda E.	WJZ-1V
Savage	Berkley A.	S. Lee Martin Co.
Schaub	Lawrence J.	Westinghouse Electric Corporation
Scher	Barry	Giant Food, Inc.
Scott	Herman	Response Group
Sears	James E.	WEBB Radio
Seward	Dolores	Maryland National Bank
Shaw	Pamela	Attorney-At-Law
Sheppard	John S.	Westinghouse Electric Corporation
Sim	Frederick	Equitable Trust Bank
Simms	Barry L.	Eastman Kodak Company
Sims	Vernon	Commercial Credit Co.
Slaughter	Kenneth	Venable, LLC
Slaughter, Esq.	Lynda	The Afro-American Newspaper Group
Sloan	Nancy	Warfield's Business Record
Smith	Joyce J.	Joy-cee Promotional Services
Smith	Judy L.	Booz, Allen and Hamilton
Smith	Kevin	American Skyline Insurance Company
Smith	Steve 0.	Kraft General Foods, Inc.
Smith	Thelma	Baltimore Urban League
Smith	Carl	C & P Telephone Company of MD.
Smith	Denise A.	WPOC, Nationwide Communications
Smith	Dwight	WMAR-TV
Smith	E. Joseph	Social Security Administration
Smith	Eugene M.	EMS Limousine, Inc.
Smith	Graylin E	Arthur Andersen & Company
Smith	Larry	Council for Equal Business Opportunity
Smith	Mitchell	Equitable Trust Company

Smith	Peter A.	Ainsworth Paint & Chemical Corporation
Smith	Zed A.	The Rouse Company
Smith, PhD.	James E.	Psychological/Consultant
Smith, PhD.	Michael	The Easterling Group
Smithery	Jeff	Office of Health Care Quality
Snow	Caroline	Consultant
Snuggs	Clarence	Maryland National Bank
Solis	Francesca	Black & Decker Company
Solomon	Allyson R.	Maryland Air National Guard
Spencer	William T.	Norton & Spencer Insurance Agency, Inc.
Stafford	Helen	Career Development Corporation
Stamp	Karen Walsh	Community Lending Group
Stamp, MBA	Darren	The Henson Company
Stanley	Harriet	C & P Telephone Company of MD.
Stephens	James D.	Charphens, Inc., T/A McDonald's
Stephens	Jerome	Stephens & Associates, Inc.
Stephens	Kenneth A.	Charphens, Inc., T/A McDonald's
Stephens	Richard H.	The New Daily Record
Stephens	Charlotta M.	Charphens, Inc., T/A McDonalds
Stewart	Janice R.	The Baltimore Sun
Stewart	Pierre	American Skyline Insurance Company
Stokes	Carl	Mid-Atlantic HealthCare
Strand	Tracey K.	National Life of Vermont
Stroud	Barron L.	Miles & Stockbridge
Stroud, Jr.	Karen	The Yarn Group
Sullivan	Carla	Graduate Student
Sullivan	Joanna	The Baltimore Business Journal
Sydnor	Samuel I.	Parks Sausage Company
Tate	Henry	Westinghouse Electric Corporation
Taylor	Karen K.	Taylor Consulting
Taylor	Melvin	Parks Sausage Company
Taylor	Leroy	Certified Public Accountant
Taylor	Rodney E.	Maryland Department of Health and Mental Hygiene
Taylor, Jr.	Kenneth R.	Montgomery County Government
Tengella	Koli	Consultant
Thomas	George	The Business Travel Center
Thomas	Janet	Johns Hopkins University
Thomas	Tammi Palmer	University of Maryland at Baltimore County
Thomas, Jr.	Lametria	Urban League
Thomas, PhD.	Dorothy	Urban Services Agency
Thompson, Esq.	Freda	US Dept. Health & Human Services
Thornton	James H.	Coppin State College
Thornton	Zerita	C & P Telephone Company of Maryland

Trigg	Jennell	National Sales Manager
Trusty	Terry L.	Marketing
Tuck	Marcia	Citizens Bank of Maryland
Tucker	Beverly C.	Shuckers Inner Harbor
Tunstall	Diane	Baltimore Gas & Electric
Vaughn	Luci C.	Piedmont'Airlines Inc
Walker	Douglas	Alex Brown & Sons
Wall	James A.	University of Maryland Medical Srvs.
Wallace	Patrice	Midian, Inc. TIA Innovation
Waller	James	Connecticut General Life Insurance Co.
Ward	John E.	Safeguard Business Systems
Ware	John C.	Maryland Hospital Services
Washington	Joseph L.	Baltimore Urban League
Watford	Nicole L.	Aspirations Limited
Weaver	Bessie M. B.	West Baltimore Community Health Center
Weaver	Pamela L.	Bell Atlantic Mobile Systems
Webster	Kenneth L.	Maryland Dept. of Housing & Community Development
Wells	Madeline	Blue Cross/ Blue Shield
West	James E.	WEBB Radio
Westbrook	Arthur	National Brewing Co.
Wheatley	Roland	Hauswald Bakery Co.
White	Marsha	The Afro-American Newspaper Group
White	Jacqueline	Consultant
Wickham	DeWayne	Vanita Productions, Inc.
Wiggins	Jonathan	Bristol-Myers Squibb Company
Wilburn	Victor	PHH FleetAmerica
Wilburn, III	Roslyn L.	Westinghouse Defense & Electronic Systems Center
Wilkes	Howard	Kangaroo Transportation Ltd.
Williams	Julie E.	Crum & Forester Commercial Insurance/Xerox
Williams	Robert J.	C & P Telephone Company
Williams	Donald	Abel Automobile Insurance Company
Williams	Gerald A.	The Chapman Company
Williams	Harold	Baltimore Gas Electric Co.
Williams	Pierre	Baltimore City Housing Authority
Williams	Rosalyn G.	Irvington Florist
Williams	Talmadge T.	Programs for Achievement in Reading
Willis	Roderick C.	Free State Information & Media Services
Wills	Julie E.	Crum & Forester Commercial Insurance/Xerox
Wilson	Benita E.	Baltimore City Department of Planning
Wilson	Cindy	Northern Acceptance Corpration
Wilson	James P.	Bethlehem Steel Corporation
Wing	Carla B.	The Bravo Group
Winstead	Mary	Rexnord Automation Corporation

Wood	John S.	Attorney
Wright	Denise I.	Provident Bank of Maryland
Wynn	Gwendolyn	Gwendolyn Century 21 /Home Specialist
Wynn	Jessie	Consultant
Yarn	Karen Braithwaite	The Yarn Group
Yarn	Steven D.	State Mutual Life Assurance Company of America
Young, Esq.	Harold D.	Law Office of Harold D. Young. P.A.
Young	Renee	
Young-Gillis	Gregory	Consultant
Yuille	James	Information Services Group

ACKNOWLEDGMENTS

First, I would like to thank my wife, Carolyn. Her patience and advice kept me focused and she was a constant voice of encouragement for me to complete the project.

Thank you to the late Ackneil M. Muldrow, II who almost daily called me during the twenty-eight years I have worked on the book. Muldrow enthusiastically and unabashedly shared volumes of his work products much of which are included in the book.

The BMA Alumni – Kenneth R. Taylor, Jr., James L. Roberts, Eugene M. Smith and Nicolas T. Abrams, permitted me to infringe on their time and patience with the final draft of the book.

Thank you to artists James E. Smallwood and Dan Houston whose illustrations bring to light the accomplishments of men and women who were inducted into The Black Business Hall of Fame.

CPSIA information can be obtained
at www.ICGtesting.com
Printed in the USA
BVHW010201161121
621757BV00003B/133